A NEW ORLEANS VOODOO
HERITAGE EDITION

DR. JOHN MONTANEE

A GRIMOIRE

The Path of a New Orleans Loa
Resurrection in Remembrance

Dr. Louie Martinié

BLACK MOON PUBLISHING
CINCINNATI, OHIO USA

Black Moon Manifesto

It is the Will and mission of Bate Cabal/Black Moon to effectively manifest unique and insightful occult Works for the esoteric community in a manner that is unfettered by commercial considerations.

© Copyright 2019 Louis Martinié (unless otherwise noted)
Design and layout © Copyright 2019 Black Moon Publishing, LLC

BlackMoonPublishing.com

Design and layout by
Jo Bounds of Black Moon Publishing, LLC

Photo Credits:
Pages 108, 111, 112, 113, 114 and 220, Louis Martinié
Page 143, © Copyright 2014 Pamela Marie Nemec

Painting of Dr. John's Tomb:
Page 109, © Copyright 1993-2014 Linda Falorio
Private Collection, Fred Fowler

Veve of New Orleans:
Page 221, Mishlen Linden

ISBN: 978-1890399-73-3

United States • United Kingdom • Europe • Australia • India

"Life is only comprehensible through a thousand local Gods. And not just the old dead ones...but living Geniuses of Place and Person!...Spirits of certain trees, certain curves of brick wall, certain chip shops, if you like, and slate roofs...Worship as many—as you can see—and more will appear!"

—Equus, Peter Shaffer

Dr. John is one of these "local Gods." Open to all who reside physically or spiritually in New Orleans.

"Also...the obeah and the wanga...these he shall learn and teach."

—Aleister Crowley, 1938

Dedication

To Mishlen Linden and our nights on the chesterfield doing art, writing, and brewing coffee. You believe in who I am able to be.

To Maegdlyn whose passion and persistence has carried this grimoire from fragment to fruition.

To DJ and to Mary Maegdlyn who first laid their spectral hands upon Gwenivere, Patrick, and I in 1973. This grimoire is a node in The Quest.

Lastly, I dedicate this work to Louis Martinié, whom I married so many years ago at my birth. He has stood me and stood with me. I have worn his face and he has worn mine. We have come to be together. Till death do us part, and then only while in time's embrace.

Acknowledgements

Thanks to all of my spiritual teachers and to all of my spiritual fiends. To Priestess Miriam of the New Orleans Voodoo Spiritual Temple who is Priestess and sister to me. To all of the temple drummers of the New Orleans Voodoo Spiritual Temple, especially to Jorge López, Robyn L. Loda, and to Mac McFarland. To Joey and to Don who live now in the drum's bright womb. To Zayin who lives in my heart.

To the voices of the community of whom I am proud to be one among many. To the voodoos at Gryphon's Nest, Babalon Rising, and Starwood. To Cliff who believes in the community and acts on his belief. To Jeff R., I will hear your voice every summer. To Sallie Ann Glassman, your dedication is an inspiration. To Dr. Marty who is always there before, during, and after the rites. To Linda Falorio and to Fred Fowler for art and insight. To Baron Sylvia and for her care of the dead loa and the Ozark Voodoo Temple.

To Mac/Dr. John, "one called to the task" who points the way. To Nema and Lairus, we travel together. To Claudia and Jon and the light Starling shines on the path. To Amzie Adams for perspective in the going.

To Madame Barbara Trevigne and Carolyn Morrow Long, all that is true in this work rests on your shoulders.

To Jo Bounds, for his patience and love. The word "thanks" is woefully inadequate.

CONTENTS

1. Beginning at the Destination 9
2. First Conjure: The Pelican 11
3. Second Conjure: Speaking in the Voice 21
4. Third Conjure: A Conjure Ball 33
5. History: Links and Talismans 37
6. Folklore: Links and Pathways 89
7. Voices of the Community:
   Experiments, Explorations, Experiences,
   Investigations, Teachings, and Conjures 115
       Festival Teachings, Conjures, and Magickal Records
           Gryphon's Nest Festivals, Louisiana 118
           Starwood Festivals 120
           Babalon Rising Festivals 124
       Experiments, Explorations, Experiences, and Conjures
           Always Listen to the Doctor
               by Claudia Williams 129
           Dr. John Montanee: The Physician's Message
               is Know Thyself by Lilith Dorsey 131

Gris Gris Lamp for Dr. John Montanee
  by Denise Alvarado 133
To Sleep On The Tomb of Dr. John Montenet
  by Witchdoctor Utu 139
Notes on the Painting of The Tomb of
  Doctor John by Linda Falorio 143
Bringing Balance to the Order of Voodoo
  Religion by Priestess Miriam 145
The Elevation of Dr. John Montane
  by Andrieh Vitimus 146
Some Conjures by Louie Martinié 148
A Dream and a Ritual Record by Maegdlyn . . 151
You Can be a Healer Now by Baron Sylvia . . . 152
He Walked From His House
  by Houngan Steven Denney 153
A Dream by Pamela Marie Nemec 154
Drum Needed to be Played
  by Midnyte Hierax 154
Sweet, Sweet Water 2012 Babalon
  Rising Festival: Conjure by Sara Terry 155
Investigations
  Bright's Disease: A Medical Investigation
    by Sara Grey 157

The Superposition of Dr. Jean: A Handwriting
    Investigation by Denise Alvarado 160
Dr. John Montanee: An Astrological Riddle
    by Rev Bill Duvendack 173
Dr. John's Natal Astrological Chart
    by Rev Bill Duvendack 180
Dr. John's Marriage Progression Astrological Chart
    by Rev Bill Duvendack 181
Sonick Sigil: Drumming Dr. John's Name
    by Vovin Lonshin and Louis Martinié 182
8. The Spiritual Doctors of New Orleans 183
9. Ending at the Beginning: Why - An Apologia . . 187
10. New Orleans: A Voodoo Pilgrimage 193
Bibliography 207
Index 213

Beginning at the Destination

History and folklore have Dr. John filling many posts. He was a freeman of color reputed to be a contemporary of Marie Laveaux in the voodoo on Congo Square, a New Orleans conjure man, drummer, herbalist, physician, and spiritual Doctor as well as having a coffeehouse and dealing in real estate. He was a man worth knowing and is a spirit worth working with.

We, all of us who participate in this Grand Working of Necromancy, can open the road for Dr. John Montanee to walk again among the living if it is his will to do so. We reach through the crossroads to the Wise Doctor of New Orleans Voodoo.

All of the pages of this grimoire exist only to help the practitioner perform the conjures with greater connaissance.

Do not feel specially appointed if the object of this conjure is successful on the first performance. Do not feel disappointed if the result is not successful on the 100th performance. Success most truly comes when the words, actions, and thoughts of the conjures become habitual, a part of who you are within any given moment. It is good to remember that success is from the root *succedere* and in its ancient usage refers to "what comes after." Something is being created that inevitably leads to something else and so on ad infinitum. How the practitioner judges his or her "success" may be quite inconsequential.

These conjures find their origin in New Orleans Voodoo.

As such the individual and his or her relationship with the loa is paramount. Change what you will. Keep what you will. Suit your self in both clothing and spiritual practice. You have a unique fit in both, too much, too little, too large, too small, all miss the mark. You know what brings you closer to spirit, loa, and deity.

There are elements of a grammar in this grimoire and attention has been directed to spellings so that the spells may be more effective. Word origins have been selectively emphasized. "The origin of words is the unconscious of language (Bob Contradino, conversation)."

The conjures are offerings to Dr. John Montanee. They are given without seeking a personal benefit. They do not ask anything of him. So many people only call to Marie Laveau to take or to find help. Consider how our friends would react if we only came to them when we wanted something.

Read and master the grammar. Do the conjures. Then listen as once dry dust takes on a new life. The facts of history are the bones. Folklore is the flesh. Conjure is the spirit. Dr. John will speak to you.

First Conjure: The Pelican

This conjure builds on the understandings, aspects, and attributes of the *New Orleans Voodoo Tarot* (Martinié, Glassman 1993), personal rituals and conjures, the workings of Bate Cabal, and the words and teachings of the ancestors.

Two rocks may be purchased or found before beginning this conjure. Black rocks or fed lodestones are the most effective. I will use lodestones in describing the conjure. Hold the stones for a time, a number of hours is best. Imbue them with your essence using sweat, blood, or other secretions you have produced. Rub them together in your palms and listen to their voice. The lodestones may be placed in a cooker, a pot with a lid used to mix ingredients for spells, the night before performing the conjure or on a full moon night (Mishlen Linden). The signature of Dr. John Montanee and a variety of talismans can be cooked with the stones. Along with these two lodestones, obtain enough rocks to construct a small pile, some earth from a graveyard, and a vial of waters. All of these ingredients can be placed in the cooker.

Preparation

Cleansing

In order that you may be purified of all that is not essence, offer your self however that self may manifest in

this exact present moment to Ti Zaraguin, or other spider loa. May your bones be picked clean that you may shine in the Visible and Invisible Worlds with a brutal elegance.

The insect loa are close and easily summoned once you have established a relationship with them. I have found that this relationship at the least includes not heedlessly taking the lives of these magnificent loas' children. If you see one of this nation in distress, help it and charge it to tell its Grandmother or Grandfather of your help. I remember a man who began the rites and was horribly bitten; it is best not to ask for more than you are willing to give. To take a being's life is to subtly invite that being to, in turn, take your life.

Assume an open stance, vulnerable, naked, head back a bit. Offer your body's midsection. With your eyes half closed and half open, create an image of a familiar spider in the dark upper half of your vision. See it move. Trill/vibrate the tip of your tongue against the roof of your mouth. This vibration of the tongue can be accompanied by high or low toning. While doing this imbue the image of the spider with two important attributes I have come to know through my possessions by the insect loa. The first being the overwhelming impulse to protect the stomach from harm. The stomach is shielded before the head. There is food being digested in the stomach, it must be protected. The second being "a fierce allegiance to life." Life is movement and even if only one small feeler or fang can be moved it will strain to perceive or attack. There is much that can be learned from the insect loa, "Never surrender, never give up" being not the least of their admirable traits.

Allow the particular self that manifests as you at this moment to be fed upon.

Dedication

Before beginning, place the two lodestones on a pile of rocks. The stones will live at the top of the pile. Manman Bridgette often sits on top of such a pile.

See Manman Bridgette in her role as a great judge. She is seated on the pile of stones. These stones are her past judgments and their firmness and fairness support her authority. One rock supports the other and the pile (or "stupa" Sanskrit for "heap") supports Manman. Such piles have been created since time immemorial to serve a variety of purposes. Now hold the lodestones, one in each hand. Rub your thumb across the stones to produce a sound.

Call to Manman Bridgette to judge and to rule in favor of this mystical work of art. Explain as a lawyer would the "why" of your conjuring of Dr. John. Your explanation will be individual, your own. That is how it must be. My successful explanations in the past have been based on community and benefit to the community. Leave the dedication with the two lodestones, confident not in your success but in her wisdom to judge fairly. At this point the stones may take on a skin-like texture. They are, in a sense, the fingers of Manman Bridgette.

An Indifference to Outcome

Place your actions and their success (in ancient usage "any outcome or result") under the governance of the most complete spiritual being that is most real to you. Again, this is individual. For me, this is the union of "my" Ti and Gros Bon Ange, the Holy Guardian Angel of Thelema, and the Buddhas of the Tibetan Bönpo Dzogchen Practices.

Each of our actions excite universes of probabilities. Let go of that which you have never had and accept the heavings and bellowings of the World Elephant, pregnant with possibilities. Choose to act for no reason. Pure will lies beyond the guttering light of "because." Reasons for actions rise and fall and crumble. They provide little stability upon which to base conjures. Call upon something more deeply rooted in the very essence of being. Do what you must.

The Pelican: First Sight

Dr. John is seen before you as in a dim light, a reflection in the glassy eye of a cat, ephemeral as a softly heard grace note in a great symphony. Indistinct as in murky waters, his figure slowly revolves with legs and arms spread, limbs falling, drifting one into the other. Closer inspection reveals a lack of vitality and both external and internal coherence. His face, while animated, shows no emotion or understanding. This is a mere apparition. There are a number of useful techniques for calling this vision. An old Magick Mirror is effective as are half closed eyes where the vision is seen in the upper, darkened part of the eye.

Pulling

During the conjure, hold a lodestone in each hand with your palms up and open in a welcoming gesture toward the apparition. With this specter of Dr. John fixed in your mind you will, "pull" him through the elements that exist within you one after another. If you are using lodestones, this pulling looks and feels like the magnetic attraction a lodestone exerts on iron. Welcome Dr. John Montanee and

invite him to pass through your body. The image will begin to move and pass into and through your body. During this passing, the powers of the chosen element flows into the specter. You are a microcosm of all the Greater and Lesser Assemblies.

Now the worker is well prepared to add strength, body, substance, and presence to Dr. John by taking his spectral self through the four elements and spirit. The alchemical pelican, as depicted on the Great Seal of Louisiana feeding its young with its own blood, is a proper image for this part of the conjure.

Earth

While holding the lodestones in the palm of the hands with your fingers, take a pinch of earth (graveyard dust is best) using the thumb and the index finger of both hands. Using the right hand, sprinkle the earth in blessing on the stone held in the left hand. Repeat the process with the opposite hand.

"Honor and Respect to Baron Samedi, Baron le Croix, Baron Cimetiere, Guedeh Nibo, Ti Jean Millipede. Lend your graces to this holy work. Give to Dr. John Montanee the weight and solidity of earth."

The apparition of Dr. John floats before you. Beckon to Dr. John with both hands in welcome holding the lodestones blessed with earth. Pull Dr. John through your body, pull him through the element of earth as it exists within you. He enters through your feet and exits through your forehead.

Here Dr. John Montanee gains a solidity of self and the virtues of earth. The purposeless spin of the apparition lessens.

Waters

Hold the lodestones now blessed with earth in the palms of your hands and dip the thumb and index finger of both hands into a chalice of water. Using the right hand, sprinkle the water in blessing on the lodestone held in the left hand. Repeat the process with the opposite hand.

"Honor and Respect to Olokun, to la Baleine, to la Siréne, to Agwe of the Waves. Olokun whisper to la Baleine, la Baleine whisper to la Siréne, la Siréne whisper to Agwe of the Waters. .Carry the Holy Name of Dr. John Montanee from the ocean floor through the abysmal waters, up through the waters that know light, to the waves, the great messengers of the sea. Agwe of the Waves carry the name Dr. John Montanee both far and wide. Lend your graces to this holy work. Give to Dr. John Montanee the fluidity and virtues of water."

The apparition of Dr. John floats before you within the aethrs. Beckon to Dr. John in welcome with both hands holding the stones blessed with earth and water. Pull Dr. John through your body, pull him through the element water as it exists within you. He enters through your stomach and midsection and exits through your forehead. If the genitals are used here as an entry point, a type of pregnancy and magickal childe may ensue.

Here Dr. John Montanee gains the delicious, moist texture of life. There is now a fluidity of self and the virtues of water.

Fire

Rub the thumb and index finger of each hand together

to produce heat while holding the lodestones blessed with earth and water in the palms of your hands. Move the heated thumb and index finger of the right hand over the left hand transferring their heat to the lodestone in the left hand. Repeat the process with the opposite hand.

"Honor and Respect to the great bearers of light, Ogun of the Forge, Erzulie with lips red as blood and hot as fire. Damballah la Flambeau bring the light and strength of your sky fire. Guedeh la Flambeau freely rain the fires of orgasm. Legba la Flambeau bring words ablaze dancing to spells falling like fiery embers. Simbi la Flambeau intellect bright bestow." He enters through your heart and exits through your forehead.

Welcome Dr. John with the heated lodestones. Pull him through your body on waves of heat. Offer the heat within your body for him to fuel a presence. The specter quickens; now it must breathe.

Air

Share your breath with the lodestones. Blow gently then forcibly upon the lodestone held in the right and then on the lodestone held in the left hand. This is a most intimate offering in that your breath is moist with fluids which contain essences individual to you alone.

"Honor and respect to le Grand Zombi (Great Serpent) bringer of magick and wisdom. Simbi impart your connaissance to heal and to curse. Nan Nan Bouclou grow herbs that heal the body, the mind, and the spirit. Legba speak the Word that opens the gate to all words."

Welcome Dr. John with words carried on the wings of air. Winds of life surround him as he passes through your

body. Offer your airs pregnant with life. He enters through your nostrils and exits through your forehead. No longer a simple specter, Dr. John stirs.

Spirit: Self Among Selves

The lodestones are now heavy with earth, water, fire, and air. An amazing and critical possibility arises at this point. The elements can mix creating a whole greater than the sum of its parts.

Bring the palms of your hands together and join the lodestones. Cup your palms loosely to form a dark space around the lodestones. This is a womb.

The two lodestones now stand as the Marassa, the divine twins from which all that is arises. The space around the twins is both empty and filled with the Waters of Return. This is not so much a contradiction as a mysterie. Creation takes place as the elements mix within these waters.

Hold your cupped hands out before you to Dr. John. Open a space between your cupped hands for Dr. John to enter this womb world. Now the Waters of Return, not you, beckon to Dr. John. The soft swirl and the security of the luminescent darkness reaches out to sooth, to gently call. Here is peace.

Here there takes place not so much an imbuing of essential qualities as a recognition (re+cognition is a "re-knowing" or to "know again") that the combination of earth, water, fire, and air can mix and create the conditions for a sentient being to exhibit not only knowledge but a special kind of wisdom commonly called connaissance which is an esoteric knowledge of and from the loa.

Move your cupped hands containing the Marassa to your forehead and then to the back of your neck. Open them a bit for Dr. John to enter through the back of your neck. Move your cupped hands once again to your forehead. Dr. John moves through your head.

Imbue Dr. John with the essence of your True Spirit. This True Spirit may manifest in many ways. Some are: Master of the Head and Holy Guardian Angel.

Imbue Dr. John with the essence of your Will which may be seen to manifest as the Ti Bon Ange, Destiny, or Ka.

Imbue Dr. John with the essence of your Love...called by some the Gros Bon Ange, Ba, Great Spirit, Goddess, or God.

During this passage Dr. John is exposed and imbued with three essences, not individual manifestations, of connaissance. This is critical in that connaissance takes on different aspects in different practitioners. It is the essential ground of connaissance which is imbued. Here it may be helpful to focus on function rather than the form that function takes.

Importantly again, Dr. John does not take on your True Spirit, your Will, or your Love. It is the essence, the fertile ground from which these great qualities arise that is shared with Dr. John. If the aspects, not essences, are emphasized, all you will have is a rather predictable and boring doppelgänger of your self.

Close your eyes, open your hands, and move out of the way. The next move, whatever that may be, is up to the Good Doctor. Place the lodestones on the pile of rocks under the protection of Manman Bridgette ready for the next conjure. If fed lodestones are used, wipe your hands

upon the earth.

End Note: While complexity has its place I much prefer a more simple and direct approach. This conjure has but few essential qualities. The conjure exists as an offering to Dr. John Montanee; not an entreaty or a command.

    The voodoo cleanses, dedicates their actions, and releases their focus from a lust for result. Dr. John is first imagined. This imagining is given substance with the elements in the crucible of the voodoo's body. In the last step a nether womb is created, Dr. John enters that nether womb and is then passed through the voodoo's head. Now it is up to Dr. John. Place the lodestones / black rocks in a jar or bag on the pile of stones for the next time the conjure is performed.

On the Waters of Mar Assi
Saint John's Eve
June 22, 1913

THE SECOND CONJURE:
SPEAKING IN THE VOICE

Abracadabra, an ancient spell, can be translated in Aramaic as "I have created through my speech"
— Denny Sargent

Words and speech are the stuff of a powerful magick. Grimoire is reminiscent of grammar. To spell (verb) and to cast a spell (noun) are quite similar in form and, in a subtle sense, meaning. Much of the "who" the mind thinks we are is composed of words and influenced by the subtleties of language.

"I think therefore I am," points to a way of being often defined and encapsulated by words and language. If "I" am to reside in this cage, then I would choose a large, more inclusive cage that allows a bit of roaming, has a view and an accessible key.

I sit at a desk and write. This "desk" does not exist except as a word. As the Tibetans say, it exists as a "nominal designation." It exists in name only. I can not find a "desk," I can not touch a "desk" only parts that break down into other parts. Office to furniture to desk to writing surface to drawers to wood to cells to atoms to. .the hereto now unrideable higgs bison to. .the practitioner's reaction to these words.

Akoko, a friend and teacher, when asked if the loa are real once replied, "They are as real as the United States of America and the United States can kill you." I would add that they are as real as this "desk" upon which I write and as real as the Dr. John conjured in this rite.

Dead Loa

The loa are sentient beings and as do all sentient beings they live, die and are reborn again and again. Their lives are tremendously long as judged by our standards and they do end. Forget (for get) literally means to lose one's grip on. A dead loa is one whose name is forgotten, no longer honored or reviled. The word, the meaning of "desk" will certainly be lost in time. At that point, desks will cease to exist. Perhaps heaps of wood and metal will litter the landscape, undistinguished from their surroundings.

I write to add my voice to the voices of those who would not permit this to happen to Dr. John Montanee. His name will not pass into this grey netherworld. His name will be remembered and honored.

Osiris

There is a beautiful precedent for this conjure. The Africans, in particular the Egyptians of Northern Africa, had a God they called Osiris. This God was murdered, his parts re-collected and then re-membered by Isis. The reanimated Osiris then impregnated Isis. It is exactly this kind of remembering that this conjure is about. Dr. John is reanimated and enters into a very intimate relationship with the practitioner.

From Recollection to Rememberance

The process is first recollection then remembrance. Recollection done in this manner flows easily into a re-membering therefore, we will re-collect Dr. John as the initial step of this conjure.

Re-Collect:

To re-collect is to collect again.

Middle English collecten, from Latin colligere, coll ct-: com-, com- + legere, to gather; see leg- in Indo-European roots.

What we collect, what we gather together, are historic and folkloric documents and references. The fertile fields from which we are collecting are composed of the materials found in the Historical and Folkloric sections of this grimoire. Collect with your head, heart, and hands. Read and feel as you hold the pages rich with ancient script. They are like carefully gathered flowers. Invite what they contain into your life. Invite Dr. John Montanee into your life.

Three Selves to Collect:

We all create at least three selves.
Me. .Records: The historical (They speak of me) is recorded in records of birth and death, in our social and business affairs. There is a sense of distance between the "they" and the "me". These are the footprints we leave upon the legal landscape that legitimize and bind. This

"Me" is close in meaning and function to the, creatively translated from the German, "superego" as described by the pioneering Viennese doctor, Sigmund Freud.

I. .Stories: The folkloric (I speak) is composed of the stories you tell about your self to your self and to others. These are also the stories your biological and social children, standing in your place, will tell about you. This "I" is close in meaning and function to the "ego" as described by Dr. Sigmund Freud.

My Self. .Assertions (from Latin *asserere* to join to oneself, from *serere* to join): The magickal (I My Self speak) is a very intimate portrait painted with one's words of a self that joins to Self by one's Word. An assertion often begins with, "By my Word. ." This "MySelf" resonates with the "id" as described by Dr. Freud.

Perspectives: Me, I, and My Self

They speak of me.
("me" becomes an object. The first person singular pronoun is *I* when it's a subject and *me* when it's an object.)
A reality observable by the other.
Superego
Objective/Scientific
Historical Perspective

I speak.
("I" is subject, the speaker.)
Firsthand accounts
Stories we create about who we are

A reality only "I" and those who reside within this "I" can create/experience.
Ego
Subjective/Personal
Folkloric Perspective

I myself speak.
("myself" intensive pronoun)
This perspective is the "self" joining with the "Self." A holy union in which the mystic can experience, the artist can create, and a loa or spirit can rest in its becoming and manifest.
Id
Projective/Creative
Conjure/Perspective

The historic (You speak of me) and folkloric (I speak) dimensions of Dr. John are included in this grimoire. The magickal (I myself speak) we will generate in this conjure.

Re-Membering

As a preliminary practice for the remembering of Dr. John, think of someone you have loved earlier in your life and have not seen for some time. How do we remember those who have passed away from us? Memories and recollections rise up. Do these memories and recollections reflect the person as they are now? If I were to see the person at this moment, I may not physically recognize them. The person, as they appear to my senses would certainly have changed. Yet the recollections create a shimmering overlay connected by a chain of cause and effect to the person who once was.

This is the ephemeral link we will feed and use in the conjure. Re-collect Dr. John in the manner Isis collected the parts of Osiris. Re-member him as Isis pieced the members of Osiris back together.

I have found this conjure to be particularly effective when performed peering into a mirror. A Magick Mirror is a mirror dedicated to not so much seeing into as to seeing through (*New Orleans Voodoo Tarot*, Martinié and Glassman, 1992, page 76). Bring together the lights and the images in your mind and juxtapose them before your eyes in the Magick Mirror. Focus. Look to the sides and then the center. The images will solidify, distort, overlay. Independent movements of the image within the mirror are a good indication that the doorway has begun to open. It is a door that easily opens.

THE CONJURE: SPEAKING IN THE VOICE

> Who Are You?
> Who Are You?
> Who Are You?
> (repeated as the cry of an owl.)

These powerful words are used to conjure the names of spirits and in a complete magick they can be used to obtain your own name.

"Who" is a questioning. A seeking, a movement. An owl beckoning the stars.

"Are" is the creation of being. Bringing the vastness of chaos to an equally vast seminal point (Kether as point).

"You" is the acknowledgement of otherness. Most awe

full in scope when applied to one's own selves.

Stare into the Magick Mirror while asking this question. The question is repeated three times as the first step into each of the three askings.

During the first asking, answer with all you have collected from History.

Respond with "I am Dr. John Montanee. You say that I. . (was born on...was born in. .married on. .married to. . and so on)."

During the second asking, answer with all you have collected from Folklore.

Respond with "I am Dr. John Montanee. I. .(drummed with. .I drummed in. .I worked conjures with...am buried in. .and so forth)."

Now quiet your present mind for a moment. Rest this mind in formless essence. From this quiet and empty space travel the road open by the responses in the first two questionings. Ask the tripartite question for the third time from a space deep within your re-membering of Dr. John. Then make this assertion for no reason, based only on the weirdness of your word.

"I am Dr. John Montanee. I greet you. .(conjurer's name). I My Self ask who are you?"

Now the question is asked of the conjurer. Close your physical eyes. Do not look into the mirror. The mirror and its images have fallen into an in-between place that the Tibetan would call a Bardo. Answer the Doctor's question with your eyes closed. Do not look into the mirror. Open your eyes to the mirror for his response. Hear from both near and afar.

This holy conversion flows into conversation. Respond to the good Doctor's question in the tone in which you

want to converse. Choose to set the tone. The End Note contains an example of this. Dr. John may question and converse with the practitioner in words or images or feelings. Repeat the cycle until the conversation is ended.

When Speaking in the Voice has waned, relax and allow the mind to rebuild a convenient self. The mind is quite good at such constructions. Give thanks, make an offering, and depart. The offering can be as simple as the heat from your hands or as complicated as a set of personally favored incantations.

It would be wise to keep an internal or external record of what is said.

When this conjure is performed effectively, it will conclude with Dr. John Montanee flowing into the form of a bud self within the practitioner. The worker is impregnated by a re-membered Dr. John much like Isis and Osiris. This bud self feeds on habit. Conjure often.

This is not so much a reversal of roles as a realization that the world is more fluid than usually imagined. The Visible and the Invisible Worlds are divided by but a thin door. Our actions, our very thoughts can cause this door to swing in both directions. The Magick Mirror can become this door. As a forgotten ancestor once phrased it, "For I am divided for Love's sake, for the chance of union."

With minor modifications, the design of this second conjure is useful in working in an array of practical situations to engender a variety of outcomes. Perhaps there is a decision of some importance that you, as a Worker, would like to influence. What better way than to become the person (Speak in the Voice of the person) who is making the decision and plant seeds that direct the actions of the person in a particular direction. This means of entry

is much more elegant than the more common, and a bit course, shredding the target's aura to gain entry.

End Note: Who Are You? . . . Our Stories

The third asking of "Who are you?" in this conjure is crucial. Now Dr. John asks this question of the practitioner. A relationship is developing. The tone of the relationship is in large measure guided by the tone of the practitioner's response. You can choose the tone in which you respond but remember that in the heat of the conjure, in the dense midst of the contact all can change in an instant. Priest Oswan Chamani of the New Orleans Voodoo Spiritual Temple consistently taught that to plan too strictly for a rite is disrespectful of the loa.

This is a record of my response to the third asking of "Who are you?" in the "Speaking in the Voice" conjure. It may be useful to the practitioner in developing the tone of the conversation with Dr. John Montanee. I have found that if we speak with a simple honesty, vulnerable trust, and heartfelt passion the loa will respond in kind. You get what you give. This is the tone that I my self prefer.

We are all from a holy place where history melts into memory which in turn cooks down to stories we tell ourselves to create our various selves.

> I am from stories of a junkie
> Who played drums
> On the Delta Queen
> As mom watched
> On the river bank with her father
> Sitting & married & sad & helpless.

He couldn't get it up
Except on the point of a needle.
I have one of his cymbals
Broken and treasured.

I am from clapboard houses
& black widow spiders
& dads who sit silent & stutter & can't talk.

I am from silence I hated
that became golden when in its arms
I heard a dove's soft songs.

I am from poets
Who argue with English professors
& wear sandals
& have beards
& have long conversations with Mom
As I sit with thick books and hope they notice
me and the books as I reach out for something I don't know
And want to share with them.

    The above is an example of such a story, in this case my story. Your story will sound different notes than mine but the melodies they form are so very similar. You can see that in my poem and you will see this in Dr. John's life.
    These melodies all revolve around our pleasures and our pains. We rise to heights on feathered wings held together by our passions, we fall when the rapture fades and doubt melts our infatuation. The acceptance of vulnerability is a kind of nakedness that often leads to a true and tested type

of strength.

Dr. John Montanee's story is no different from ours in its essence and this essence forms a road on which we can greet him as fellow travelers. All perceptions are selective and memory has a large yard in which to play. Dr. John's remembrances, his large yard, is now peopled with historical facts, the tales of folklore, and the spirits of conjure. It is a goal in this grimoire to include enough of the facts and folklore and conjure that the good doctor can reach into the practitioner's soul and tell his own story with no help.

We would do well to embrace Dr. John's humanity before reveling in his presence as a loa. "We are the most universal when we are the most personal." This quote from Ursula K. Le Guin illuminates an elusive facet of what it means to be universal. The ancient cabalists wrote of "revolving" an idea in order to examine it from all angles. My approach to the life and afterlife of Dr. John Montanee invokes this type of revolving. This grimoire revolves the personal in order to allow Dr. John to manifest in a most universal manner, as a loa. Here passion is an apt measure of authenticity if not mundane (mundus) accuracy.

Third Conjure: A Conjure Ball

The first and second conjures move in the realms of action and speech. The Pelican conjure focuses on actions, movements, and objects to serve Dr. John. The Talking in the Voice conjure relies heavily on the use of speech to bring Dr. John through. A Conjure Ball, the third calling, takes place in mind/spirit. There is a movement among the conjures from action to speech to mind/spirit. This can be seen as a movement from complexity to simplicity. There is no better or worse, higher to lower in these conjures. It would be best to experiment with all three and continue with the one(s) which is most effective for you. Also, it would be unwise to forget that these are but three of many ways to the desired end. .the quickening of Dr. John Montanee as a loa if that is his will.

Directing the Mind to its Intended Target

While it is the simplest of the three conjures it is perhaps the most difficult to perform in that there is no sensory input to aid in directing the mind to its intended target. The body does not move. The mouth does not speak. Nothing moves but the mind. A major value to be found

in the minimal form of the third conjure is that it can be performed anywhere.

AIM AND TENSION: THE BOW STRING IS TIGHTENED

Fill your head with all the information one can find about Dr. John. Fill the heart to the brim with all of the feeling Dr. John evokes in you. Imagine moving your hands in actions that you associate with the Doctor, possibly drumming or constructing herbal cures and curses. The heart leaps at the play of sights, sounds, and actions. It smiles at the world created in the mind.

RELEASE

Relax your mind, heart, and hands when they are bristling with friction, at the moment of their maximum intensity. Colors and shapes cascade into a place of stillness. They collapse and coalesce into a tight conjure ball. A black hole that pulls the microcosm you have created into an unimaginable tightness.

CONTACT

Move the ball to the tomb of Dr. John Montanee in St. Louis Cemetery No. 1 and/or to St. Roch Cemetery. The ball explodes in a beautiful display, like fireworks over the city seen from a levee. Offer the beauty and grace of this display to Dr. John Montanee.

An End Note to the Practitioner: The three conjures are

acts of service to Dr. John Montanee. Ask nothing of him, expect nothing of him. Be quiet. Listen and see and sense what arises.

History: Links and Talismans
The Objective View

These documents are presented as links and talismans. They are tendrils reaching back into the space/time occupied by Dr. John Montanee. Revel in the shapes of the letters, the subtle interplay of space and ink. The forms of the documents are links firmly set in time's fabric. Use them to enter a New Orleans now lost in the thick mists of dark swamps and bayous. The content of the documents, in particular the signature of Dr. John, is well suited to talismanic use. The documents are given to the practitioner to use and their "use" is of paramount importance. If they serve the three conjures, then their function is most adequately addressed.

I know of no historical documents definitely connecting Dr. John Montanee to the drums or to Marie Laveau though there are definite folkloric references to such connections. What we call "history" is a filter used to organize perceptions and it is important to remember that all perception is selective. Visual focus is a good example of this. We do not see all that is in front of us. We select what we consider to be important and focus on that small section of the available visual array.

One need only remember the early critiques of feminists focusing on "his-tory and her-story" to realize that history can also be very selective in its content. In addition, a famous

dictum states that "history is written by the winners" and the conditions for winning may consist of things as simple as knowing the right people or luck. It can be helpful to recognize that objectivity is something to be attained rather than a given in historical studies. Most definitely, not something to be taken for granted.

That being said, the spirits and loa have provided the chance to rely heavily on the exacting work of Carolyn Morrow Long and the ground breaking work of Barbara Trevigne. It is truly by the grace, persistence, and knowledge of Barbara Trevigne, Carolyn Long and other like researchers that these and many other documents were recalled from obscurity and eventually oblivion.

Carolyn Morow Long's thorough research into the figures of New Orleans Voodoo gives the historical section of this grimoire an integrity not otherwise possible. Her discovery of John Montanee's signature and her kindness in taking me to the Notarial Archives Research Center to see and to make copies of his signature has and will continue to benefit generations of drummers in the Spiritual Houses and Voodoo Temples of New Orleans. Madame Barbara Trevigne's research, writings, and first hand contact with the spirits is a blessed font from which flows both wisdom and knowledge. She is the first to uncover and make available through publication definitive information regarding Dr. John Montanee's life including his marriage, his burial, and his children. Her article reproduced here is an inexhaustible source of both facts and avenues of future investigations. She is a living talisman connecting all of us to Marie Laveau and to Dr. John. To these two I would add, Maegdlyn Morris who provided inspiration and piercing intellectual insight in the gathering of all of the grimoire's

materials. In addition, so much of this grimoire would have been lost to Hurricane Katrina without Maegdlyn's numerous interventions.

There is much more than a simple finding or discovery here. The loa and spirits smiled and a gate opened through which the documents could be recalled by those chosen for the task.

The Documents

It was only within the last decade or so that the majority of these documents were brought to light. This is an amazing and exciting fact. New Orleans Voodoo is a living, growing spiritual practice and these documents contribute to its resilience and vitality.

The documents follow a general chronological order. A transcription of selected sections of some of the original documents is provided where the original text may be difficult to read. The text in italic is not found in the original document. Italicized text in "Selected Transcriptions" and "Selected Entries" is meant to clarify, render unreadable text accessible, or suggest possible avenues of thought and inquiry.

DrJohnVoodoo.com is sponsored by Black Moon Publishing and is a nexus dedicated to making all of our ongoing experiments, explorations, experiences, investigations, teachings, and conjures available to practitioners. The material in this section will be available on the Dr. John Voodoo website. In addition the documents in the historical section will be available for download on the website as high definition jpeg files.

I would encourage all, in particular lovers of New Orleans

and its history, herbalists, voodoos, and drummers to be a part of this research through additions to or comments upon these documents. DrJohnVoodoo.com as well as BlackMoonPublishing.com are funded by a private trust fund and as such will be available to all in perpetuity.

No.
Jany 1847
.. sale of
land
by
Montane
to
Egli

United States of America
State of Louisiana
City of New Orleans

Be it known that on this Fifteenth day of January Eighteen hundred & forty Seven, in the 71st Year of the American Independence.

Before me, Octave de Armas, a notary public in & for the Said City of New Orleans, duly commissioned & sworn, and in the presence of the witnesses herein after named & undersigned.

Personally came & appeared Jean Montane, Senr, residing in the said City, unmarried; Who declared that by these presents, he doth sell, bargain, transfer & deliver, with all legal warranties, & with substitution & subrogation to all his rights & actions of warranty against his own vendors or authors

Unto George Egli of the same City, herein present & accepting, purchasing for him, his heirs & assigns, and acknowledging possession thereof.—

Two certain lots of ground Situate in fauxbourg Tremé, in the First Municipality of this City, designated as Numbers twenty five & twenty Six of the Square bounded by St Peter, Roman, Ursulines & Hospital Streets, agreably to a Plan drawn by L. Bringier & deposited in the office of H. Pedesclaux (now C. V. Foulon) notary public of this City, in his Book

gage by him permitted in favor of his vendor,
Louis Mathil Rampon Chedister, to secure the
payment of two hundred & twenty five
dolls, as appears by the above recited act of
22nd March 1846, before S. I. Mouissan, not.
(of which mortgage the present purchaser has
-mised the reduction as aforesaid to the amounts
One hundred Dollars.) & for the commission On
hundred & twenty-five Dollars, release thereof sh
be hereinafter granted; 4rd: And the
version which the said Isaac Marcelous has
by the same act on the stead of heir of this ve
of the Original mortgage granted by
said H. J. Chedister in favor of Anthony
wonder, to the amount of three hundred
ninety five Dollars, according to an act by
Nomidia Ducatel, not pub, dated the 6
September 1845, — of which mortgage relea
same after be fully granted. ————

———— That the said George Eyd.
is a holder of the two following notes, which are a
provision to no. the reality duly annexed, to
a note for One hundred & twenty five
dolls, drawn by H. J. Chedister to his own order,
the 17th September 1845 & payable Nine month
date — Signed & accepted the same day, by
said Notary Amidée Ducatel, & 2nd. another
note for One hundred & twenty five dol
drawn by Isaac Marcelous to the order of the s
Chedister, dated the 22nd March 1846, & pay
Six months after date — Signed Marcelous, a
same day, by the said notary L. I. Mouisseau
—————— Declares (the said G. Eyd.) the
their presents he does fully & to the amount of s
notes, release the mortgages & recession of
Mortgage which secure the payment of
notes, & which are fully recited in the Cer
ficate of the Recorder of Mortgages, he
annexed. ————

———— Thus done & passed at the C
of New Orleans, on day of the said notary's
five, on the day & year first above rec

of Plans No. ... Plan 11th ; - Which
Lots are adjoining, & measure each viz.
No. 25.= Thirty feet in front on Prairie
by about Sixty five feet in depth. the
line measuring thirty one feet two in
& one line, & and Lot No. 26.- measure
also thirty feet front on Prairie Street
Sixty feet in depth, & thirty one feet
inches & one line, in the rear; ———

——— Together with all & singu
the improvements & advantages thereunto
belonging, the rights & privileges apper-
-taining to the same, without exception
reservation whatsoever; ———

——— The above described & com
Lots of ground are the same which
said Jean Marotani acquired by pu
-rchase from Vidal Prosper Chabotte
-cording to an act executed on the Een
first day of March Eighteen-hundred
& forty Six, before Louis T. Mau
then a notary public of this City; —

——— The present Sale is made
for & in Consideration of the price of
of three hundred Dollars, whereon the
purchaser has personally paid cash, in
-rent money of the United States, One
hundred Dollars to the said Vendor who
hereby acknowledges the receipt thereof;

——— And for the balance of the
price, say: Two hundred Dollars, the
said purchaser 1st Has subscribed to the
order of said vendor, a promissory note
of two hundred Dollars, dated this day
payable one year after date; - Which n
after being signed "ne varietur" by me, the
Notary, was immediately delivered to the
vendor who does hereby acknowledge
receipt thereof. 2nd & also the said purcha
hereby binds himself to pay, in the lieu &t

of said ___ ___, a promissory drawn by
the latter in favor of the Recorder of the said
F. P. Schmidtiller, his ___, for One hundred Dollars, dated the 25th March 1846
& ___ ___ ___ ___ ___ Date, secured by
___ mortgage on the above described
& conveyed property, as appears by the
above ___ ___ of the 25th March 1846
before the ___ ___ Louis P. ___
The said George Egli ___ ___
by these presents, the ___ of ___ ___
gage in question & that of said J. Montani._____
_____ And ___ ___ the punctual
payment of the ___ ___ ___ by
the said G. Egli, as ___, together
with an ___ ___ at eight ___ cent per
annum, if not ___ paid without
any ___ being ___ ___ to delay
___ ___ of ___ ___. The said
Geo Egli does hereby ___, mortgage
& hypothecate in favor of all ___ of
said debt, the ___ ___ ___ lots
of ground & appurtenances. ___ Promising
not to sell or ___ any part of said
property to the prejudice of the ___
stipulated mortgage, & being also ___
that the present act do bear ___
of judgment & ___ ___._____

_____ To have & to hold the
above described conveyed premises, unto
the said George Egli, his heirs & assigns, to their proper use & behoof forever, by virtue hereof._____
_____ According to the Certificate
of the Recorder of Mortgages, in & for the
City & Parish, bearing ___ date herewith & hereto annexed, the following mortgages are recorded against the said Jean
Montani, on the herein above described
conveyed property, to wit: 1st. M. most-

the presence of Messrs. Jesus Pascadis So-
laire & Jacko Baranowsky, accompanied with
us for this thing in the said City. Who
have hereunto signed their names with the
said parties & me, the Notary, after due
reading /———————————————————

Observation: Before Signing these presents,
the said George Egli has paid Cash, in
current money, to the said Jean Montanve, who
acknowledges the receipt thereof, the sum
of One Hundred Dollars which he (the said
Geo. Egli) had subscribed to the order of
the said Jean Montanve, pay able One year
after date, as above mentioned ;— So that
the Mortgage which was to secure the
payment thereof, becomes null & void /—

Jean Montanve

George Egli

Document One
Transaction Record with Dr. John Signature

Five pages
January 15th, 1847. . "Be it known that on this. ."
Recalled By: Carolyn Morrow Long; circa 2002
Source: Octave de Armais, January 15, 1847, Courtesy of New Orleans Notarial Archives.

Comments
• This is the record of a transaction.
• Dr. John Montanee's signature is the first of the signatures on the concluding page.
• Note the spelling that he uses for his signature.

Jean Maurane

Jean Maurane

Jean Maurane

Jean Maurane

Jean Maurane

Jean Maurane

Jean Maurane

Document Two
Dr. John Signature

One page
Enlarged signature of Dr. John Montanee
Recalled By: Caroloyn Morrow Long; circa 2002
Source: Octave de Armais, January 15, 1847, Courtest of New Orleans Notarial Archives.

Comments
This page is an enlargement of Dr. John Montanee's signature as found in Document One. It is of great use as a talisman in conjures opening the path to communication with Dr. John. I would deeply recommend not asking anything of Dr. John in these communications. Simply, freely offer what you can. The Good Doctor will respond.

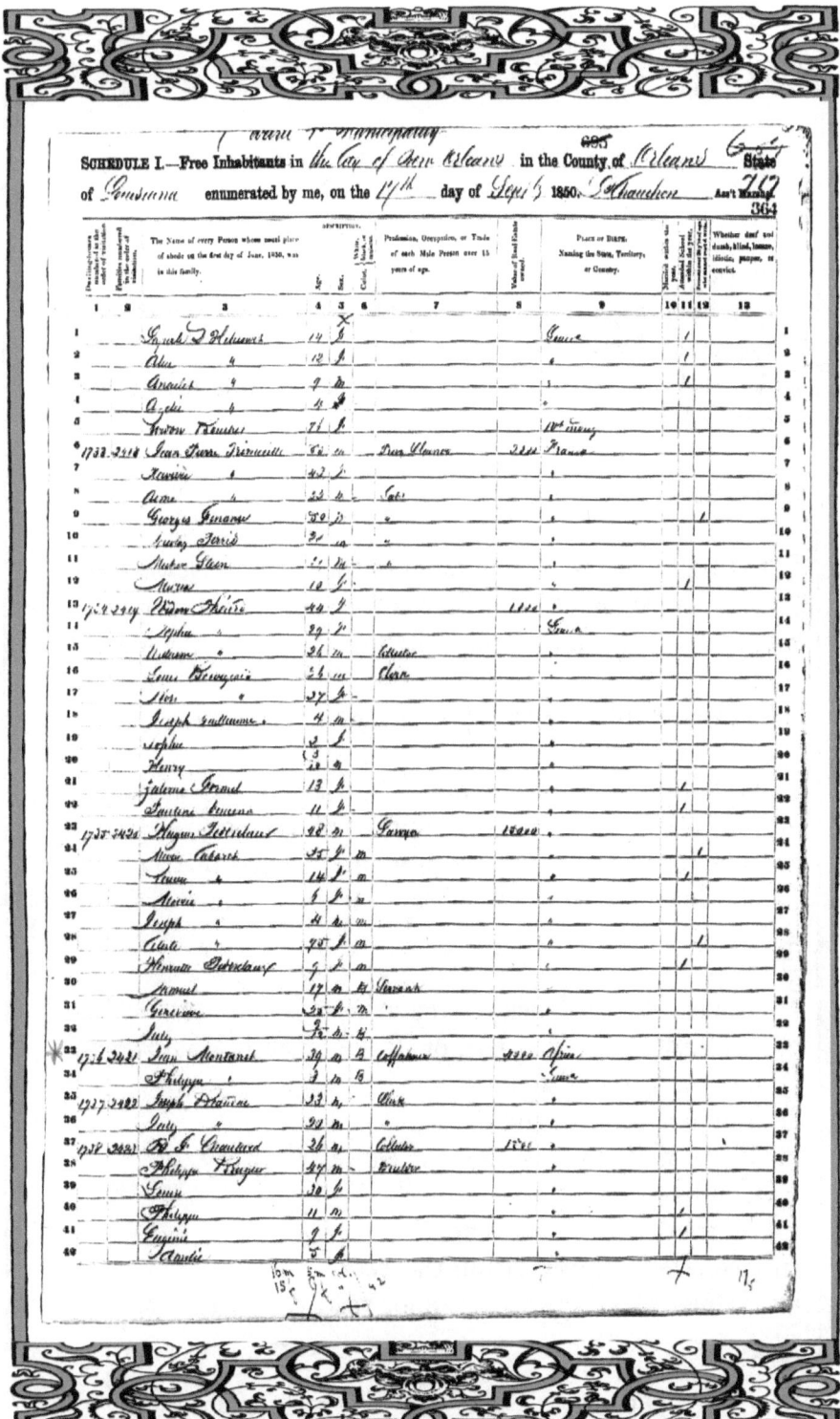

Document Three
US Census, 1850

One page
September 17, 1850.. "Schedule I -- Free Inhabitants in the City of New Orleans.."
Source: United States Census of 1850, microfilm, New Orleans Public Library

Selected Transcriptions:

Schedule I -- Free Inhabitants in the City of New Orleans in the County of Orleans State of Louisiana enumerated by me, on the 17th day of Sept 1850, Chauchon Ass't Marshal.

The twelve columns at top of page:

1. Dwelling-houses (numbered in the order of visitation).
2. Families (numbered in the order of visitation).
3. The name of every person whose normal place of abode to the first day of June, 1850, was in this family.
4. Age
5. Sex
6. Color: White, black, or mulatto
7. Profession, Occupation, or Trade of each Male Person over 15 years of age.
8. Value of Real Estate "".
9. Place of Birth, Naming the State, Territory, or Country.
10. Married within the year.
11. Attended School within the year.
12. (?) over (?) of age who cannot read & write.

13. Whether deaf and dumb, blind, insane, idiot, pauper, convict.

Selected Entries:

Line Number 33
Column 1: 1726
Column 2: 2420
Column 3: Jean Montenet
Column 4: 34
Column 5: m
Column 6: B
Column 7: coffeehouse
Column 8: 4080 ? in the thousands
Column 9: Africa

Line Number 34
Column 1: . .same as Jean Montenet
Column 2: . .same as Jean Montenet
Column 3: Philippe
Column 4: 3
Column 5: m
Column 6: B
Column 9: Louisa

COMMENTS
• Records only the "Profession, Occupation, or Trade of each Male Person." Females not recorded. This is the milieu in which Marie Laveau worked and lived.
• Columns 11 and 12 emphasize literacy. Dr. John worked on writing his name (*A New Orleans Voudou Priestess*, Carolyn Morrow Long, University Press of Florida, pg. 145).
• Philippe is a son.

- In this period, "coffeehouse" could be a euphemism for brothel.
- The present Dr. John (John "Mac" Rebennack, Jr) said, "I actually got a clipping from the Times Picayune newspaper about how my great-great-great-grandpa Wayne was busted with this guy for runnin' a voodoo operation in a whorehouse in 1860. (Wiccapedia) " The date of this document is 1850, this is an interesting collaboration of the Present Dr. John's account.
- Dr. John was well to do in the dollars of that period.

Page No. 5

SCHEDULE 1.—Free Inhabitants in _____ in the County of _____ State of Louisiana enumerated by me, on the 12th day of July, 1860. _____ Ass't Marshal.

Post Office New Orleans

Dwelling	Family	Name	Age	Sex	Color	Profession	Value Real	Value Personal	Place of Birth	M	S	A	Remarks
1470	1823	A. Adams	38	m		Clerk ✓							
		Adele	30	f									
		Adele	9	f									
		Virginia	7	f									
		John	5	m									
		Catherine	8	f					Ireland				
1471	1824	Isaac Isaac	34	m		Tailor ✓		400	France				
		Rebecca	26	f									
		Nycia	6	m									
		Solomon	4	m									
			3	f									
			7/12										
		Benj Isaac	23	m		Pork ✓		180	France				
1472	1825	Mr Kohn	39	m	Im		2700	600	La				
		Alex	27	f	Im								
		Louis	4	m	Im								
1473	1826	Edw Magit	30	m		Auctioneer ✓		1800	France				
		Alice	28	f					La				
			1	f									
		Alice	2	f									
		Catherine Welsh	20	f					Ireland				
1474	1827	Eugene Duffez	40	m		Comm Merchant ✓		300	La				
		Natalie	29	f									
		Anne I.H. Voris	19	f			2100						
		Bridget Jr. Mendes	24	f									
		Edmond	4	m									
1475	1828	M. Pedesclaux	62	m		Notary ✓	13000	800					
		Celestine Francois	40	f	Im								
				f	Im								
		Leo											
		Louis Pedesclaux	18	f									
			98	f									
		Pierrette	14	f	Im								
		Remi	6	f	B								
1476	1829		30	m		Dry Cleaner ✓		1250	France				
		Marie	16	f					La				
		I.	3	m					La				
		Louis Haas	42	m		Dry Cleaner ✓			France				
			31	f									

No. white males 6 No. colored males 2 No. foreign born ___ No. blind ___ 17,500 8,000
No. white females ___ No. colored females ___ No. deaf and dumb ___ No. paupers ___ No. insane ___

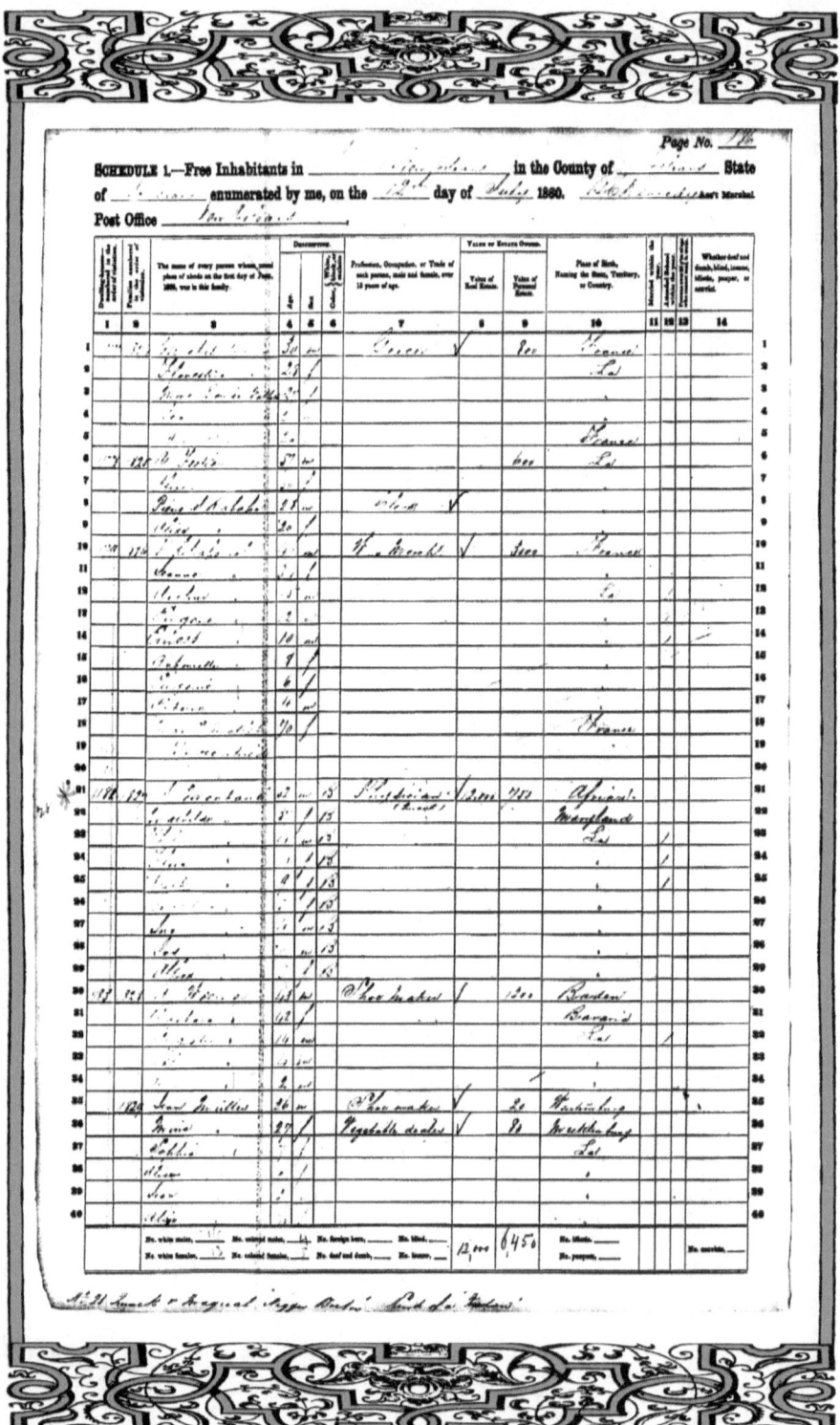

Document Four
US Census, 1860

Two pages
July 12th, 1860. . "Schedule I — Free Inhabitants in ? New Orleans. ."
Source: United States Census of 1860, microfilm, New Orleans Public Library

Selected Transcription:

The twelve columns at the top of page:
1. Dwelling-houses — numbered in the order of visitation.
2. Families numbered in the order of visitation.
3. The name of every person whose normal place of abode on the first day of June, 1860, was in this family.
4. Age
5. Sex
6. Color: White, black, or mulatto
7. Profession, Occupation, or Trade of each person, male and female, over 15 years of age.
8. Value of Real Estate.
9. Value of Personal Estate.
10. Place of Birth, Naming the State, Territory, or Country.
11. Married within the year.
12. Attended School within the year.
13. Free(?) over (?) of age who cannot read & write.
14. Whether deaf and dumb, blind, insane, idiot, pauper,

convict.
Selected Entries:

(Page 2 of 2)
Line Number 21
Column 1, 1182
Column 2, 1827
Column 3, J Montane
Column 4, ?2
Column 5, m
Column 6, B
Column 7, Physician (under "Physician" appears to be the word "Quack")
Column 8, 12,000
Column 9, 750
Column 10, Africa

Line Number 21
Column 1,
Column 2,
Column 3, Mathilde Montane
Column 4, 37?
Column 5, f
Column 6, B
Column 7, No occupation is listed
Column 8,
Column 9,
Column 10, Maryland

Lines 23 through 29
These lines list the children living in the household with the surname Montane. Three are male and four are female. Two females and one male attended school within the year.

All of the children were born in Louisiana.

COMMENTS:
• Column 7 now records the Profession, Occupation, or Trade of free males and females. In 1850 only free males were recorded.

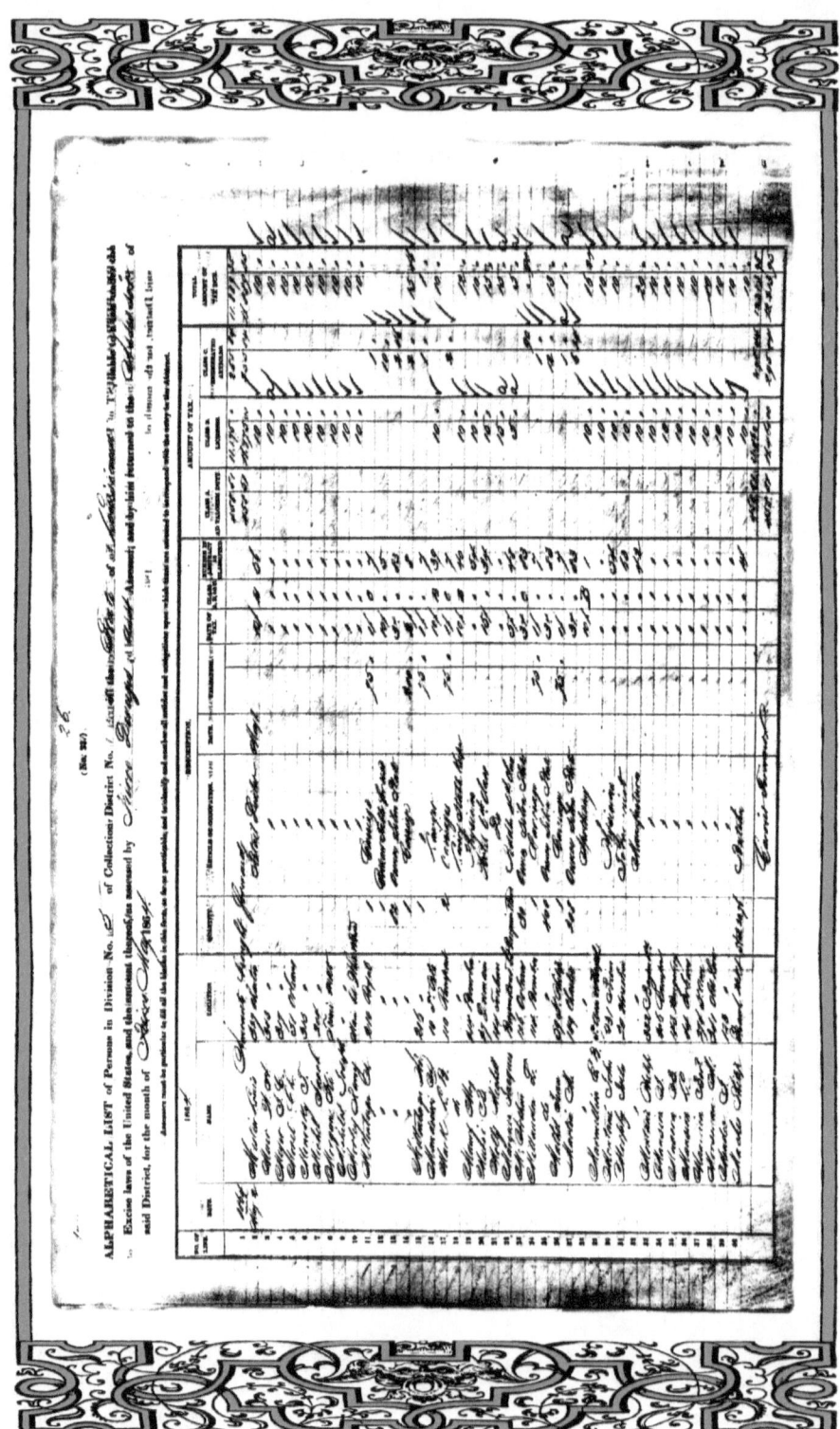

Document Five
Collection District List, 1864

One page
May 2nd, 1864.. "ALPHABETICAL LIST of Persons in Division No. 5 of Collection District No.1 State of Louisiana.."

Line 30. ..Montané, John with Physician as Occupation. The Location is not readable. 231 Prieur?

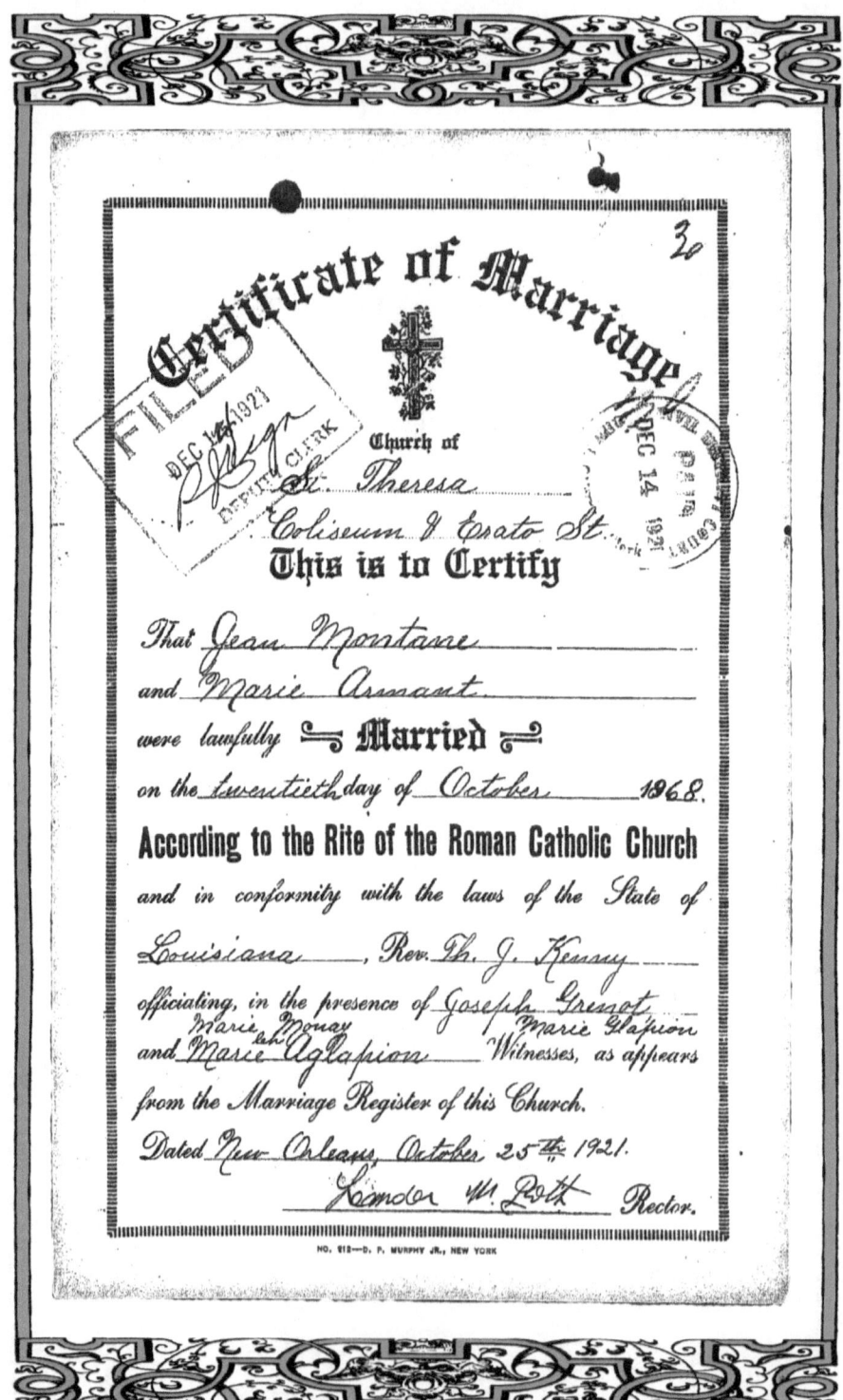

Certificate of Marriage

Church of St. Theresa
Coliseum & Erato St.

This is to Certify

That Jean Montane
and Marie Armant
were lawfully **Married**
on the twentieth day of October 1868.

According to the Rite of the Roman Catholic Church

and in conformity with the laws of the State of Louisiana, Rev. Th. J. Kenny officiating, in the presence of Joseph Grenot, Marie Monay and Marie Aglapion, Marie Glapion Witnesses, as appears from the Marriage Register of this Church.

Dated New Orleans, October 25th 1921.

Lander M. Roth, Rector.

Document Six
Certificate of Marriage

One page
December 14th 1921. ..Certificate of Marriage
Recalled By: Madame Barbara Trevigne
Source: From documents pertaining to the Succession (Document 9)

This is a copy of the original certificate.
"Jean Montane and Marie Armant were lawfully married on the twentieth day October 1868." Note that Marie Glapion is listed as a witness. This could be a connection with Marie Laveau in that she had Christophe Glapion as a domestic partner and mothered 7 children with him.

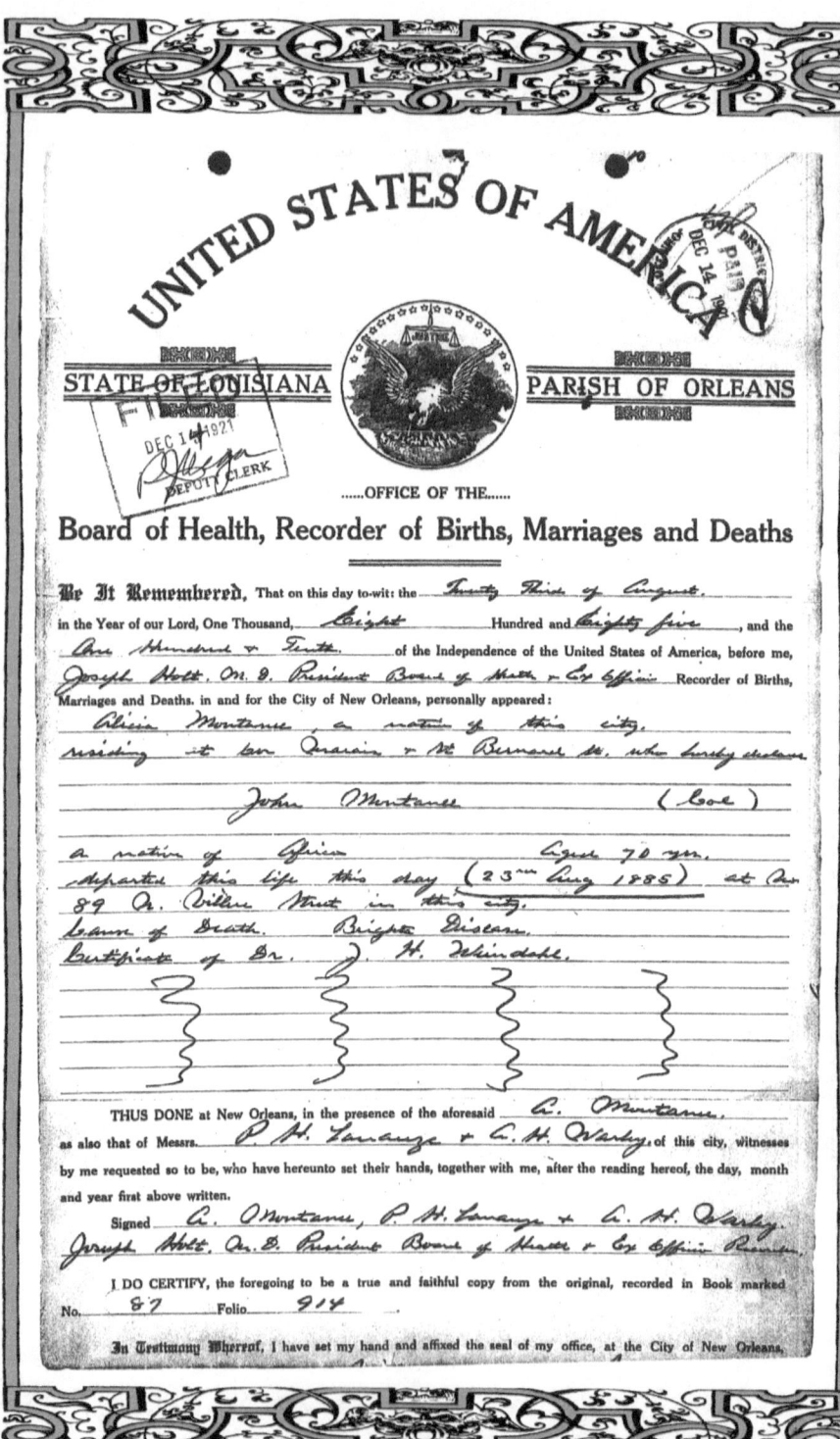

Document Seven
Certificate of Death

One page
December 14th, 1921. ..Certificate of Death
Recalled By: Madame Barbara Trevigne
Source: From documents pertaining to the Succession (Document 9)
(Original – New Orleans Public Library, microfilm, Vol. 87, p. 914)

This is a copy from the original certificate. Hand written text toward the middle of the page states that "John Montanee a native of Africa Aged 70 yrs., departed this life this day (23rd August 1885) at (?) 89 N. Villere in this city. Cause of Death. Brights disease. "A. Montanee" is the first signature on the certificate.

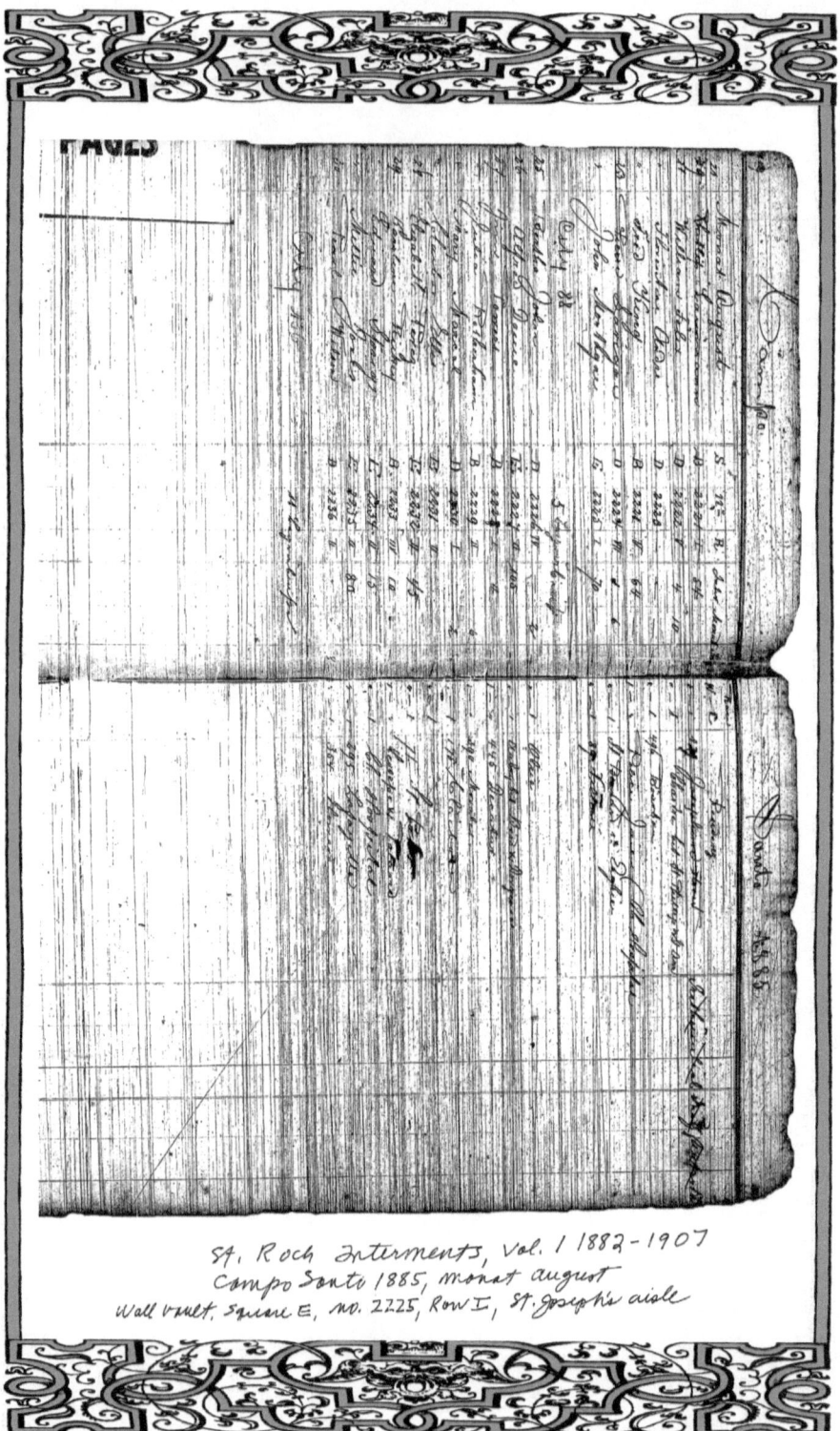

St. Roch Interments, Vol. 1 1882-1907
Campo Santo 1885, month August
Wall vault, Square E, no. 2225, Row I, St. Joseph's aisle

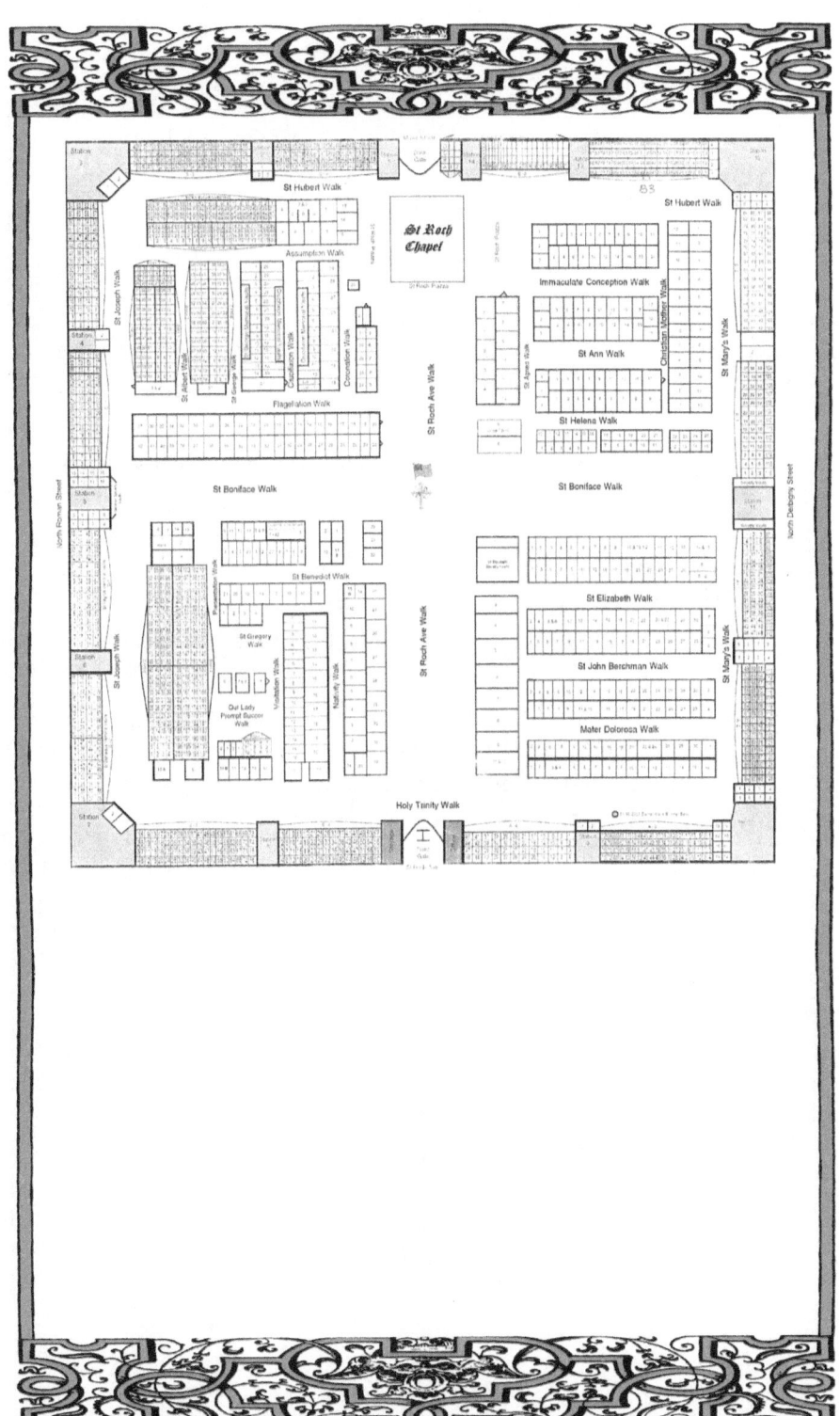

Document Eight
Interment Record and Map of Cemetery

Two pages
Interment Record
Source: Cemetery Interment Records, Saint Roch Cemetery, microfilm, New Orleans Public Library, Vol. 1, 1882 - 1907

Page one is a copy of the original record with a note attached.

Seventh line from the top reads:
John Montanee   E   2225   1   70   89 Villere
The attached note explains these letters and numbers.

Page two provides the layout of St Roch Cemetery.
The location described by in the interment record has not been found to date due to rebuilding and events such as Hurricane Katrina. The search is ongoing.

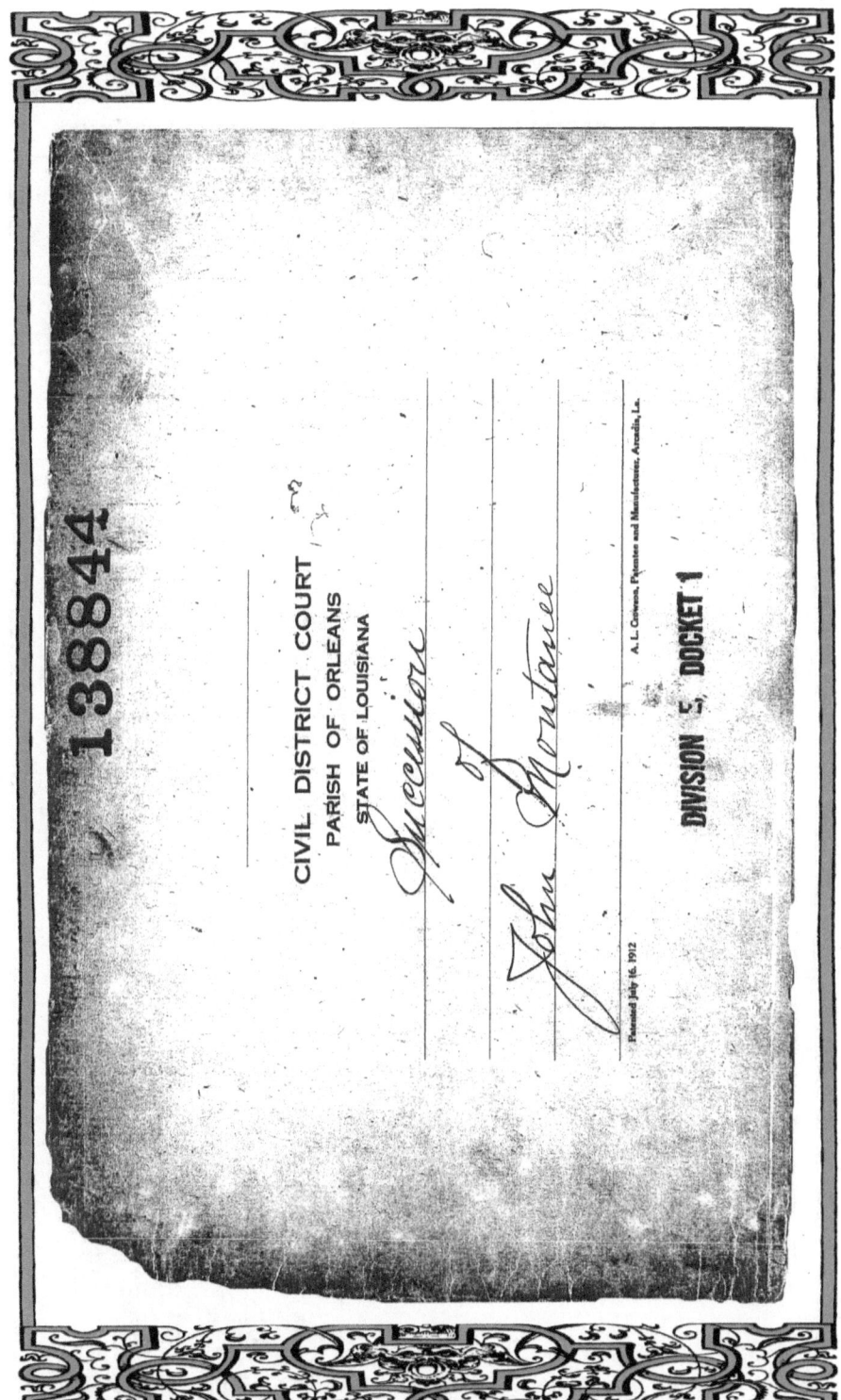

CIVIL DISTRICT COURT FOR THE PARISH OF ORLEANS,
STATE OF LOUISIANA.

NO. 133844   DIVISION E   DOCKET NO.

SUCCESSION OF JOHN MONTANEE.

PETITION FOR LETTERS OF ADMINISTRATION.

DEPUTY CLERK.

TO THE HONORABLE, THE CIVIL DISTRICT COURT FOR THE PARISH OF ORLEANS, STATE OF LOUISIANA:

The petition of THOMAS C. NICHOLLS, JR., of full age and a resident of this City, with respect represents:

1.

That he is the duly qualified Public Administrator for the Parish of Orleans, and as such, Curator of vacant estates.

11.

That JOHN MONTANEE, of full age, departed this life intestate, at his residence and place of domicile in this City, on the 23rd day of August, 1885; that the decedent has left property situated within this Parish and State; that there are privileged and ordinary debts due by the estate of said deceased, which render an administration thereof necessary; that petitioner desires to be appointed Administrator of this estate, and to have Letters of Administration issue to him upon his complying with the requisites of the law.

111.

Petitioner further represents that the deceased has left no heirs who reside in the State of Louisiana, or anyone who claims his succession, and that an attorney at law should be appointed to represent the absent heirs.

1V.

Petitioner further represents that an inventory of this estate, descriptive and estimative, should be taken, in the manner and form prescribed by law.

-2-

WHEREFORE, petitioner prays that his application for Letters of Administration on the estate of the decedent be published, according to law; that, after all legal delays have elapsed, Letters of Administration issue to petitioner upon his complying with the requisites of the law, and that an inventory, descriptive and estimative, be taken in the manner and form prescribed by law, by PIERRE D. OLIVIER, Notary Public, of this City, and that an attorney at law be appointed by the Court to represent the absent heirs of the deceased, and,

For all general and equitable relief.

_____
PUBLIC ADMINISTRATOR FOR PARISH OF ORLEANS.

_____
ATTORNEY FOR PUBLIC ADMINISTRATOR.

STATE OF LOUISIANA.
PARISH OF ORLEANS.

THOMAS C. NICHOLLS, JR., being duly sworn, deposes and says, that he has read the foregoing petition, and that all of the facts and allegations therein contained are true and correct, to the best of his knowledge, information and belief.

_____

Sworn to and subscribed before me, this 4th day of Octor, 1921.

_____
NOTARY PUBLIC.

ORDER.

Let the petitioner's application for Letters of Administration on this estate be published, according to law, and let the inventory herein prayed for be taken by PIERRE D. OLIVIER, Notary Public,. in the manner and form prescribed by law, and let _____ and _____ be and they are hereby appointed as appraisers to value the property and effects to be inventoried, and let _____, Esquire, Attorney at Law, be appointed to represent the absent heirs of the deceased.

_____
JUDGE

New Orleans, La. Octob 6th, 1921.

138844

14th October, 1921.

INVENTORY

in

the Matter of
the Succession
of
JOHN MONTANEE

UNITED STATES OF AMERICA,
STATE OF LOUISIANA,
CITY OF NEW ORLEANS.

FILED
OCT 20 1921
John Daly
DEPUTY CLERK

Be it known, that on this 14th day of the month of October in the year of our Lord one thousand nine hundred and twenty-one.

That by virtue of an order of the Honorable the Civil District Court for the Parish of Orleans, dated New Orleans, October 6th, 1921, rendered and signed in the matter entitled "Succession of JOHN MONTANEE", bearing the number 138,844 of the docket of the said Court and directing me, Notary, to take an inventory of all the property and effects belonging to the estate of the said deceased, as the same appears by reference to a certified copy of the said order of court hereto attached and made a part hereof.

Before me; PIERRE D. OLIVIER, a Notary Public, duly commissioned and qualified in and for the Parish of Orleans, State of Louisiana, therein residing and in the presence of the witnesses hereinafter named and undersigned, came and appeared:

First: THOMAS C. NICHOLLS, JR., Public Administrator for the Parish of Orleans, and curator of vacant estates, applicant for Letters of Administration herein;

Second: Robert R. Sauzier and Charles Cunee, both of full age and domiciled in this Parish, appraisers appointed by said order of court and duly sworn in such capacity, to value and appraise the property to be herein inventoried;

Third: Emile Pense, Attorney-at-Law, appointed by the said order of Court to represent the absent heirs of the deceased herein;

Fourth: Sumter D. Marks, Jr. and J. Oswald Walker, both of full age and domiciled in this Parish, competent witnesses, hereto required,

did proceed to take a true and faithful inventory of all the property and effects belonging to the estate of the said decedent, as the same was pointed out and designated to me, Notary, for that purpose, as follows:

REAL ESTATE

THREE CERTAIN LOTS OF GROUND, together with all the rights, ways, privileges, servitudes and advantages thereunto appertaining and belonging, situated in the Third District of this City, in Square No. 794, bounded by Independence, Roman, Pauline and Derbigny Streets, designated as Lots 4, 5 and 6, which said lots adjoin each other and measure 31.20. on Independence Street by 95 ft. in depth between

-2-

parallel lines; Lot No.4 being situated at a distance of 95 ft. from the Corner of Independence & Essmi, and Lot No. 6 being situated at a distance of 155 ft. from the corner of Independence and Derbigny Streets.

Being part of the same property which the said JOHN MONTANEE Acquired by purchase from FELIX M. JACOBS, as appears by act passed before A. Barnett, Notary Public, dated Nov. 28th, 1851, and registered in the Conveyance Office in Book 55, Folio 258.

Which said property is hereby appraised by the said appraisers at the sum of Nine Hundred Dollars 00/100 ($900.00), being at the rate of Three Hundred Dollars 00/100 per lot.

And the said Thomas C. Nicholls, Jr., in his said capacity, having declared that he knew of no other property or effects belonging to the estate of the said JOHN MONTANEE to be herein inventoried and appraised, I, the said Notary, have closed the present proces-verbal of the said inventory, which I have caused to be signed by the said appearers, appraisers and witnesses who have signed hereto with me Notary after due reading of the whole.

(The Original is Signed)

WITNESSES:
  Sumter D. Marks, Jr.,
  J. O. Walker

Thos. C. Nicholls, Jr.,
    Public Administrator.
R. E. Saucier,
Chas. Cuneo,
Emile Pomes.

Pierre D. Olivier,
  Notary Public.

I certify the above and foregoing to be a true and correct copy of the original inventory in the matter of the Succession of JOHN MONTANEE on file and of record in my office.

State of Louisiana }
Parish of Orleans   }

          Marie Armant widow of Jean Montane, residing at No.3051 Grand Route St.John being duly sworn did depose and say:

  That she was married to Jean Montane at St.Theresa Church a(Coliseum and Erato Strs)in this City, on October 20th,1868; that he was married but once and then to your affiant; that she has not re-married since the death of her husband; that her husband died in this City, on August 23d,1885, and was buried in St.Roch Cemetery in this City; that he left no will, so far as she knows;

  That there were eight children born of the marriage between her and Jean Montane — Four of the children died in a infancy, named Albert; Antoine; John and Marie Montane; four children lived to age of 21 named Jeanne Montane; Edward Montane; Oscar Montane and Joseph Montane;

  That Oscar Montane died in this City, August 31/01 ; he was I think married, but did not live with his wife, and had no child or children —

  That Joseph Montane died in this City, on July 5/1904 ; he was never married and left no descendants

  That Jeanne Montane and Edward Montane are still living and they are the only surviving children and forced heirs of the late Jean Montane, and only surviving issue of the marriage between affiant and said Jean Montane. —

        That she had been informed by her said husband that he owned property, or lots of ground, in the vicinity of Macarty Square but she did not know the exact location of same — that her husband was known by everybody under name of "Doctor John" as he treated numerous persons with "herb cures" —; that she never knew of any relatives of her husband

Sworn to and subscribed before   Mrs. Marie X Montane
me, October 26th, 1931   her mark

         Edward Montane being duly sworn did depose and say: that he is the son of the late Jean Montane; that all the facts in the above affidavit made by his mother are true and correct; that he has read the same and knows the facts personally, except that he does not remember any of the children who died in infancy except Mary or Marie Montane; that Joseph died unmarried and Oscar left no children of his marriage, as he did not live with his wife — that he is 48 years of age

Sworn to and subscribed before   Edward Montane
me, Notary, October 26th, 1931 —

State of Louisiana)
Parish of Orleans)   Widow Marie Troullier, residing at No. 1548 No Roman Street in this City, being duly sworn did depose and say: that she is 65 years of age; that she knew the late Jean Montane and his family intimately; that she knows his wife Marie Armant who is still living; that he died in this City many years ago, may 30 or 35 years; that he was buried from Villere Street between Conti and St. Louis; that they had about 7 or 8 children, four of them died in infancy, but four reached 21 and over; that two of them named Oscar and Joseph Montane died; Joseph was never married but Oscar was married and had no children; that there are only two children of the late Jean Montane still living named Edouard Montane and Jeanne Montane; that the deceased Jean Montane was known by every body as "Dr. John Montane"

Sworn to and subscribed before me, Notary, this 31st. day of October 1921 - - - -

Wid Troullier

State of Louisiana
Parish of Orleans

Gustave H. Goinelle, being duly sworn did depose and say: that he lives at No. 1824 Onzaga Street; that he knew the late Jean Montane very well; knew him before his marriage to Marie Armant; that he was married only once and then to Mary Armant; he was much older than the said Marie Armant when they married; she was a young woman; that the said widow of Jean Montane is still living at 3051 Grand Route St. John; that there were a number of children issue of the marriage between said Jean Montane and his wife; that they have all died and he did not know them so well, but does know that only two of the children are living, whom he knows very well, and they are Edward Montane and Jeanne Montane; that Jean Montane was known as "Dr. Jean"; that he died many years ago -

Sworn to and subscribed before me, Notary, October 31st 1921 -

Succession) No. 138.844 = Civil District Court
Of) Docket 1 - Div. "
John Montanee) Filed December 14th, 1921

Putting in Possession:-

To the Honorable the Civil District Court for the Parish of Orleans

The petition of Marie Armant widow of Jean or John Montanee; Edward Montanee and Miss Jeanne Montanee, all of full age, residing in this Parish

Respectfully Represents:-

(1) That Jean Montanee, husband of your first named petitioner and father of your other petitioners, died in this Parish, intestate, on Aug. 23/85; that he was married but once and then to your first named petitioner on October 20/68. -

(2) That there were 8 children issue of said marriage - 4 of whom died in infancy; the other 4 were named Oscar; Joseph; Jeanne and Edward Montanee

(3) That Oscar Montanee died in this City, intestate, on August 31/01 that he was married, but there was no issue of the marriage; and his sole and only heirs are your above named petitioners.

(4) That Joseph Montanee died in this City, on July 5/04, intestate; that he was single and left as his sole and only heirs your above named petitioners. -

(5) That the said John or Jean Montanee owned at his death the following described property (his separate estate) to-wit:-

Three Lots of Ground, with all rights, ways, etc. situated in the Third District of this City, in square 794, bounded by Independence, Roman, Pauline and Derbigny Streets, designated by the Nos. 4, 5 and 6, measuring each 31 feet front on Independence Street by a depth of 95 feet - lot 4 is situated 93 feet from Roman Street and lot 6 is situated 155 feet from Derbigny Street -

Acquired by deceased by purchase from F.M. Jacobs by act before A. Barnett, late Notary, dated November 28/51 (C.O. Book 55 folio 258) - - -

(6) That the Public Administrator has applied for letters of administration on this estate; that the deceased left no debts collectable at this time; that petitioners have arranged to pay the charges of the Public administrator and he has consented to their being put into possession, and so has the Attorney for absent heirs, as will be seen by their written consent affixed hereto

W H E R E F O R E, the premises and annexed affidavits and consent being considered petitioners pray that they be recognized as the sole and only heirs of the said John or Jean Montanee and Joseph and Oscar Montanee; that they be sent and put into possession, as owners, of the above described property in the proportion of 2/16 to the said Widow Marie Armant Montanee and 7/16 each to the said Jeanne and Edward Montanee, and for all general relief. - - - -

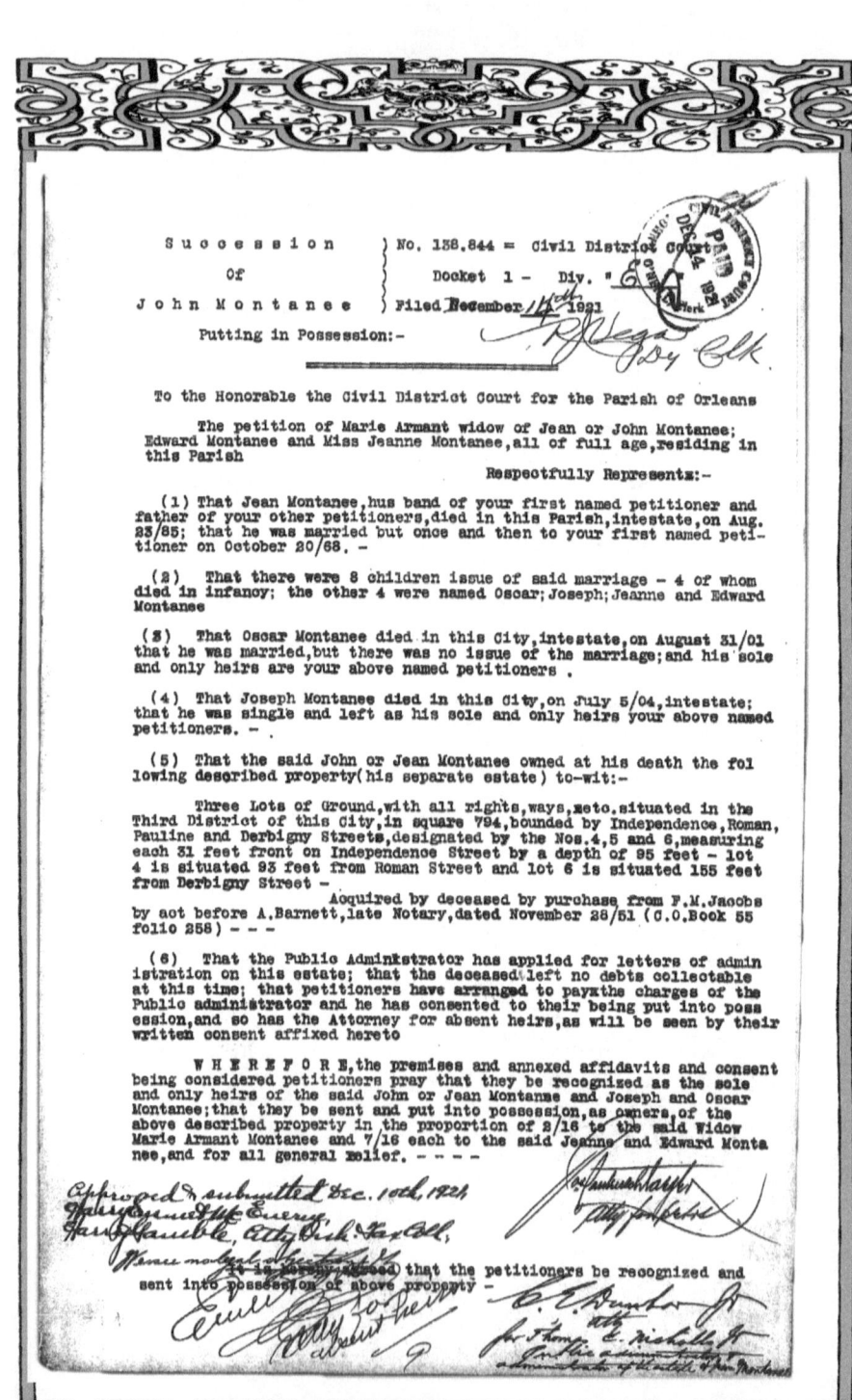

Succession) No. 138,844
Of) Civil District Court
John Montanee) Div. " 6 "

JUDGMENT: ---

On petition of sole and only forced heirs to be recognized and put into possession, no inheritance tax being due, and considering the consent of the public administrator and attorney for absent heirs,

IT IS ORDERED, ADJUDGED and DECREED that Miss Jeanne Montanee and Edward Montanee, living, and the deceased Joseph Montanee and Oscar Montanee be deceased be and they are hereby recognized as the sole and only children and forced heirs of their deceased father John or Jean Montanee.

IT IS FURTHER ORDERED, ADJUDGED and DECREED that Mrs. Marie Armant widow of said John or Jean Montanee, and the said Miss Jeanne and Edward Montane be and they are hereby recognized as the sole and only forced heirs of the said Joseph and Oscar Montanee, deceased sons of said John or Jean Montanee, and as such the said parties are hereby recognized as the sole owners of, and sent into possession, in the proportion of 2/16 to the said Mrs. Marie Armant widow of Jean or John Montanee and 7/16 to each of the said Miss Jeanne and Edward Montanee, of the following described property to-wit:------

Three Lots of Ground, with all rights, ways, servitudes, privileges and advantages thereunto belonging, situated in the Third District of this City, in square 794, bounded by Independence, Roman, Pauline and Derbigny Streets, designated by the Nos. 4,5 and 6, measuring each 31 feet front on Independence Street by a depth of 95 feet, ebtween parallel - lines. - Lot 4 is situated 93 feet from Roman Str and lot 6 is situated 155 feet from Derbigny Street - - - -

Acquired by John Montanee by purchase from F.M.Jacobs, by act before A.Barnett, late Notary, dated November 28/51 (C.O.Book 55 fo. 258)

Judgment read, rendered and signed, in open Court, December 14th 1921.

Judge

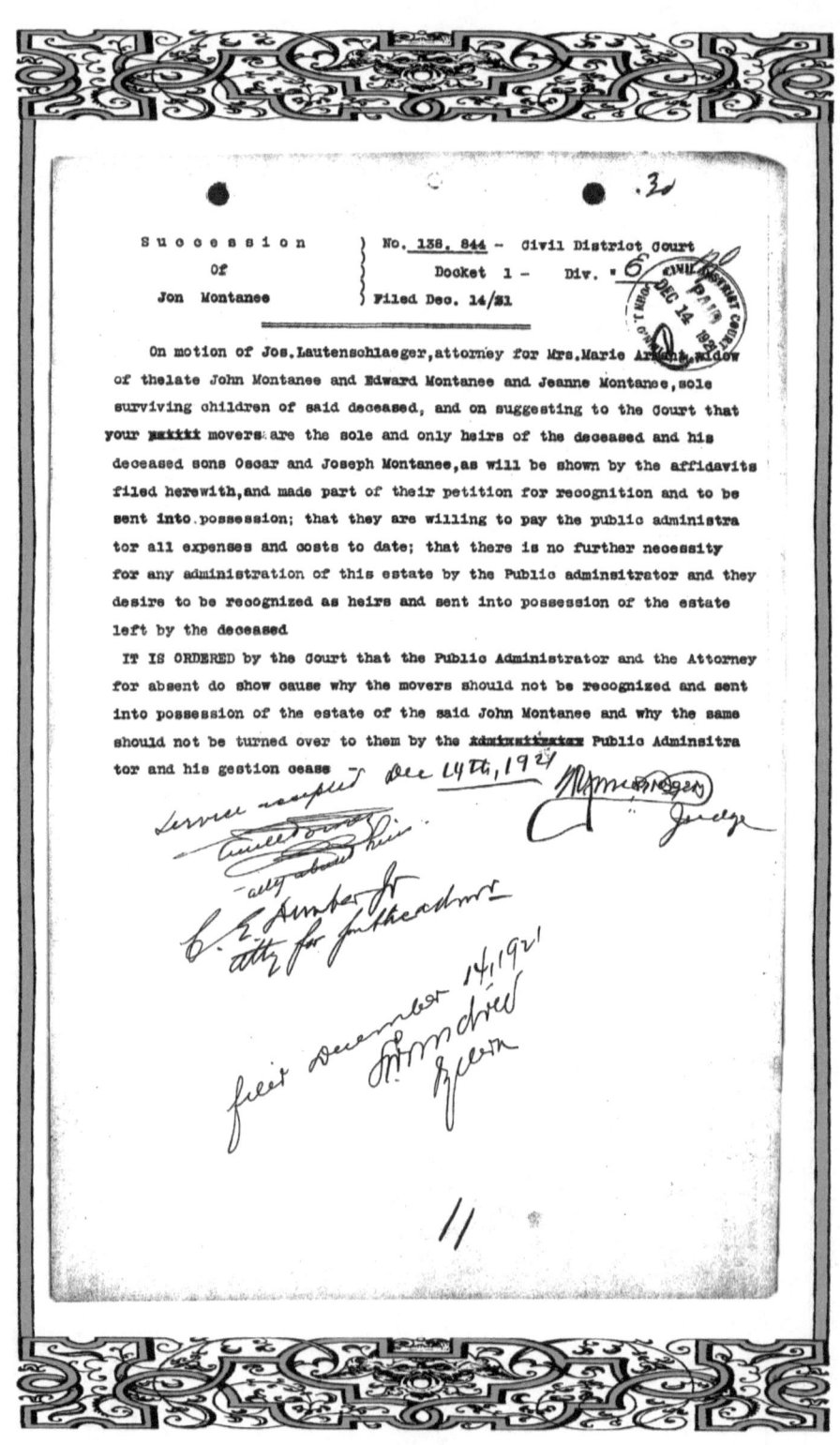

Succession) No. 138,844 - Civil District Court
Of   )   Docket 1 -   Div. "6"
Jon Montanee) Filed Dec. 14/21

On motion of Jos. Lautenschlaeger, attorney for Mrs. Marie Arnaud, widow of the late John Montanee and Edward Montanee and Jeanne Montanee, sole surviving children of said deceased, and on suggesting to the Court that your movers are the sole and only heirs of the deceased and his deceased sons Oscar and Joseph Montanee, as will be shown by the affidavits filed herewith, and made part of their petition for recognition and to be sent into possession; that they are willing to pay the public administrator all expenses and costs to date; that there is no further necessity for any administration of this estate by the Public adminsitrator and they desire to be recognized as heirs and sent into possession of the estate left by the deceased.

IT IS ORDERED by the Court that the Public Administrator and the Attorney for absent do show cause why the movers should not be recognized and sent into possession of the estate of the said John Montanee and why the same should not be turned over to them by the Public Adminsitrator and his gestion cease.

Document Nine
Succession of John Montanee

Ten pages
Succession of John Montanee, October 6th, 1921 to December 14th, 1921
Recalled By: Madame Barbara Trevigne
Source: Civil District Court, Parish of Orleans, State of Louisiana
138844, Division E, Docket 1, microfilm, New Orleans Public Library

This succession was pursued 36 years after Dr. John Montanee's passing.

This document is critical to the practitioner in that it legibly lists Dr. John's children, facts from their lives, addresses of houses, and other information that can be used to build a relationship with Dr. John. Decades ago, when working with Marie Laveau, I would recite lists of her children's names and facts from her life before inviting her to occupy a chair that was kept empty for her in our house temple.

BALL OF CONFUSION: CÉLESTIN GLAPION AND THE GLAPION FAMILY OF LOUISIANA

Submitted by Barbara Trevigne

THE GLAPION WOMEN AND DR. JOHN

There have always been stories of the Widow PARIS' association with Dr. John. Dr. John was a Voodoo practitioner, who dispensed a hodgepodge of treatment for whatever ailed you. We only know his name was John MONTANEÉ, and he was African by birth. On census records, and various other documents his surname appears as Montanent, Montaine, Montanée, and Montanet. The United States Census for 1850, 1860, 1870 and 1880 enumerated John MONTANÉE's occupation as an Indian Doctor. The date of Dr. John's exact arrival in New Orleans is unknown. However, by the time he reached New Orleans he allegedly was a free man. Based on his age when he died, he possibly was born in 1815. At seventy, Dr. John died intestate on 23 August 1885 at 89 Villere Street. His cause of death was Bright's disease, a disease of the kidneys. Upon Dr. John's death, nineteenth-century writer, Lafcadio HEARN felt New Orleans lost the last influential

man of mystical powers. Except for old newspaper articles, little is known of the cures and remedies of Dr. John, and the men who dispensed their services. These men were called Conjure Men, Voodoo Men, and Doctors. They were thought to be Two-Headed, or born with a veil [caul], meaning they could see in the spirit world and physical world. The more popular name for a male practitioner in New Orleans during this period was Doctor. Unlike José Joffry VERBOIS, a free black of the Guinea Coast, who in 1799 noted in his testament several persons owed him for his services as a healer, we have no journal or list of clients from Dr. John.[71]

Contrary to previous nineteenth-century literature, Dr. John died a literate man, who achieved some prosperity as a property owner. The earliest transaction of his identity and his cursive signature appeared 6 February 1847. Carolyn Morrow LONG, in *A New Orleans Voudou Priestess*, cites a Civil Court suit record regarding Nancy ST. MARTIN, f.w.c. and John MONTANÉE. "In her statement, she [St. Martin] maintained she is an ignorant and illiterate woman, and she was prevailed upon by Jean MONTANÉE, with whom she lived in concubinage, to make him a donation [in the form of a simulated sale], of the above property, under the promise that she would continue to be in possession thereof... and that he would... support her... in case of sickness, old age, or infirmity." The sale was declared null and void, and Dr. John was ordered to pay Nancy ST. MARTIN seven dollars a month rent from the time of the sale until she regains possession of the property, plus $300.00 damages and court courts."[72] Yet, when Nancy ST. MARTIN died, John MONTANÉE was still living at 405 Annette, when he appeared before the recorder of

deaths to provide information regarding Nancy's death. Like Dr. John, Nancy was African by birth. She died at a house on Bourbon Street between Ursuline and St. Phillip, currently the 1000 block of Bourbon.[73]

Beginning in 1843 through 1860, Dr. John was purchasing and selling real estate property and slaves. His single largest real estate purchase was in 1851. At that time, Dr. John purchased six lots for sixty dollars from Felix Morris JACOBS. These streets are currently Independence, Pauline, Roman and Derbigny. By 1857 his name appears as Jean MONTANÉE for tax assessment. At that time he had an empty lot, on Bayou Road, in addition to three houses on Bayou Road and Prieur Street. That property was located near the former site of the House of Joy bar owned by the deceased Roy GLAPION, Sr. Dr. John also owned four slaves, valued at two thousand-six hundred dollars.[74]

According to the 1880 United States Census for Orleans Parish, John MONTANET (MONTANÉE) was seventy-nine. His wife Armantine MONTANET (Marie Armantine Armant MONTANÉE), a black female was twenty-eight. The five children in the household identified as black were Marie MONTANET, age twenty-one, Arthemise MONTANET, age nineteen and a seamstress, Edward MONTANET, age eight and at school, Oscar MONTANET, age four, and Philogene a black male age one. Census information compounds confusion in identifying his family of procreation with his children named in his succession record and from sacramental records. For example, Our Lady of Sacred Heart marriage records indicates François MARTIN married Catherine MONTANÉ, daughter of Jean MONTANÉ and Mathilda WILLIAM, and Alicia

MONTANÉE in 1885, served as depondent regarding the death of Dr. John. Another child, John MONTANÉE, Jr. is identified as the son of John MONTANÉE and Marie POPULAS on his death certificate.[75]

The 1880 census recorder indicated Dr. John's son, Oscar MONTANÉE's birth, circa 1876, based on his age from the census. However, Oscar's death in 1901 at age twenty-two would place his birth in 1879. Dr. John's age by the same 1880 census recorder would place his birth circa 1801. It is obvious Marie MONTANEÉ and Artemise MONTANEÉ indicated in the household could not be children of Dr. John with Marie ARMANT, born circa 1852 by census information. In all probability, Dr. John probably fathered Marie MONTANÉE and Artemise MONTANÉE with a woman other than Marie ARMANT. There is the possibility Philogene died in infancy, yet a P. MONTANÉE appears as depondent for the male infant Jean MONTANÉE's death certificate. This infant died within twenty-eight days of birth. Thus far, I have only been able to substantiate nine children for Dr. John, including his namesake John MONTANÉE, Jr. who died in 1876 as an infant.[76]

The only known legal marriage of Dr. John was to Marie ARMAND/ARMANT. Dr. John and Marie ARMAND were married 20 October 1868, in St. Theresa Catholic Church, located on Coliseum and Erato Street in New Orleans. John WELLS and A. ABRIEL swore to the Justice of the Peace they were acquainted with John MONTANEÉ and Marie ARMAND. The celebrant was Reverend Theodore J. KERNEY. The witnesses were Joseph GRENOT, Marie GLAPION, Marie MONAY and Marie A. GLAPION. Since Lizette's daughter, Marie GLAPION was deceased; the identity of this Marie

GLAPION is unknown. The Widow PARIS is eliminated as Marie GLAPION, because she is not identified in her usual manner as the Widow PARIS. On the other hand, another witness Marie A. GLAPION, could certainly have been Ann Marie GLAPION. The identification of Marie MONAY is unknown. Although vital records are inconclusive on the Montaneé lineage, the most definitive source in reconstructing Dr. John's life was his succession. Without his succession, other contemporary writers were unable to provide a full treatment of his life in their literary work about Marie LAVEAUX, and early twentieth century writers were not interested in fact. Dr. John was of little interest to nineteenth and early twentieth century writers, except to portray him as a buffoon. He was of little significance other than to Lafcadio HEARN.[77]

There is a thirty-six year span in the paper trail from Dr. John's death until his wife and two surviving children, Edward MONTANEÉ and Jeanne MONTANEÉ filed a petition in Civil Court years after his death. On 14 October 1921 the children filed as rightful legal heirs, to obtain ownership of their father's property. From the testimony of depondents in his succession, Marie ARMAND would have been a very young woman of sixteen when she married Dr. John, a mature, shrewd man compared to her life experiences.

Immediately in question of Dr. John's estate was his lots. This property was located in the Third District, Square 794, bounded by Independence, Roman, Pauline and Derbigny Streets. The property was regulated as a vacant estate. The property was illegally sold on 9 May 1921 for unpaid taxes for tax years, 1880-1918, to the Puritan Land Company. Motions were filed, petitions written and

sworn affidavits were taken. The Civil Court judgment of 6 September 1922, ordered the State Tax Collector for the Parish of Orleans, to annul the records of "unknown," for tax years' 1880 to 1918, because Dr. John's name (John MONTANEÉ), was recorded in the conveyance office. In the end, the purchaser redeemed the property to the Montaneé family rather than stand suit.

According to Marie ARMAND's deposition, she was Dr. John's only legal spouse and did not remarry after his death. Eight children were born to their marriage - four of the children died in infancy, they were, Albert, Antoine, John, and Marie. Four children lived to age twenty-one. They were Jeanne, Edward, Oscar, and Joseph. Oscar and Joseph MONTANEÉ died in New Orleans. Oscar died 31 August 1901. Although Joseph was married, he had no known children. Joseph died 5 July 1904. Jeanne MONTANEÉ, and Edward MONTANEÉ were the sole surviving forced heirs, of their father. [78]

Marie ARMAND MONTANEÉ further testified that her husband informed her of property he owned near Macarty Square. However, she did not know the exact location. She stated everyone knew her husband by the name Doctor John, because he treated numerous persons with herb cures. She stated she never knew of any relatives of her husband.[79] Edward MONTANEÉ corroborated his mother's affidavit. For his part, Edward stated he was forty-eight years of age. Edward did not remember any of his siblings who died in infancy except Mary or Marie MONTANEÉ; that Joseph died unmarried, and Oscar who did not live with his wife, left no children from his marriage. The Widow Marie TROULLIER and Gustave H. GOINELLE were two witnesses called to provide a deposition.

The Widow Marie TROULLIER, residing at 1548 North Roman Street, was sixty-five at the time of her testimony. She would have been eleven years old when Dr. John married and twenty-four when he died, based on her birth circa, 1857. Marie TROULLIER stated she knew Dr. John and his wife intimately. Troullier indicated, "Dr. John had been dead for thirty or thirty-five years, and that he was buried from Villere Street between Conti and St. Louis. Dr. John and Marie had about seven or eight children, four who died in infancy, and four who reached twenty-one and over. There were two surviving children, Edward MONTANÉE and Jeanne MONTANÉE. Troullier's final statement was, "everyone knew John MONTANÉE as Dr. John MONTANÉE." [80]

Gustave H. GOINELLE, resided at 1824 Onzaga Street. Goinelle testified he knew the late John MONTANÉE very well, and knew John before he married Marie ARMANT. He further stated Dr. John was married only once, and then to Marie ARMANT; she was a young woman when they married; his widow was still living at 3051 Grand Route St. John; he knew Edward and Jeanne MONTANÉE very well; that John MONTANÉE, was known as Dr. John; that he died many years ago. [81]

Dr. John was perhaps New Orleans last, full blooded African living in America in post Civil War New Orleans. Part of his life was in a house on Annette Street and at 89 North Villere Street, located between St. Louis Cemeteries One and Two. When he married, the ceremony was in a Catholic church in the American sector of the city. There are no records showing when he arrived to New Orleans, or an obituary that celebrated his life. Dr. John's certificate of marriage is the only evidence that connects two Glapion

women in his life, other than Marie LAVEAUX. Notarial records indicate he was literate and did not die a poor illiterate man. From his wife's account and testimony from two witnesses, people in New Orleans sought his curative powers as an Herbalist. He was called Dr. John by his clientele, and a Quack Doctor and Indian Doctor by census recorders.

Since Dr. John was of the Catholic faith, he received rites and rituals of Catholicism. He was accorded burial in a Catholic consecrated cemetery. Dr. John's relic lies in Section E, Row One, in a wall vault in the Campo Santo, St. Roch Cemetery. Perhaps, there was some truth when it was said, "St. Roch Cemetery is by far the most *Voodist* cemetery in New Orleans." [82]

The author would like to thank, Karen Livers, Greg Osborn, Jack Belsom, Sam Reine, Gerri-Turner Warren, Doreen Troullier, Shelia Prevost, Eugenia Foster Adams, the Staff of the Notarial Archives, the Archdiocese of New Orleans Archives, the Louisiana Division, New Orleans Public Library, Lois Washington, and Kathryn Labat for their assistance.

finis

Endnotes

[71] Death certificate of John Montaneé, Recorder of Deaths, filed 23 August 1885, date of death 23 August 1885, microfilm, vol. 87, p. 914, NOPL. The death certificate was filed by Alicia Montanee, a native of this city who declared John Montaneé, a native of Africa age seventy, died at 89 N. Villere of Bright's Disease. Lafcadio Hearn, "The Last of The Voodoos," *Harpers Weekly*, reprinted Frederick Starr, ed., *Inventing New Orleans: Writing of Lafcadio Hearn*, Jackson University

Press of Mississippi, 2001. Dr. Kimberly Hanger, who did extensive research on the Colonial period in New Orleans before her untimely death, refers to José Joffry Verbois. Hanger, Kimberly S., *Bounded Lives, Bounded People, Free Black Society in Colonial New Orleans, 1769-1803*, Duke University Press, Durham & London, 1997.

[72] Ibid. Carolyn Morrow Long, n.2.

[73] Death certificate of Nancy St. Martin, age about sixty, Recorder of Births and Deaths, recorded 3 May 1834, vol. 14, p. 264, microfilm, NOPL. We have no way of knowing if Dr. John cared for Nancy as ordered by the court. He was still living on Annette and Urquhart when Nancy St. Martin died, 27 April 1834. Nancy died at a residence on Bourbon Street, between Ursuline and St. Phillip. In the 1850s, 1100 Bourbon would have been 244 or 245 Bourbon Street. Constant Landreaux, f.w.c. who had a child for this author's paternal fourth great-grandfather, Joseph Treviño, sold John Montaneé two lots facing St. Philip, Acts of Charles Victor Foulon, Notary, 03 April 1845, act 103, vol. 16, NONA. Constance Landreux's, daughter Gertrude Trevigne was half-sister of Franrçois Paulo Treviño, the author's paternal third great-grandfather.

[74] Act of Sale, Felix Morris Jacobs to John Montaneé, f.m.c. lot no, 1, 2, 3, 4, 5 and 6 of Square No. 34 by the property of L.B. Macarty, in Faubourg Washington, Third Municipality, bounded by Independence, Prosper (North Derbigny) and Solidelle (North Roman) and lots 1, 2, 3, 4, 5, 6, 7, 8, 9, 10 and 11 in Square 43 in Faubourg Washington bounded by Elmire, Congress, Célestin, and Genie Street in Suburb Washington, Acts of Alphonse Barnett, Notary, 28 November 1851, act 582, NONA.

[75] United States Census for New Orleans, Jno. Montant 1880, p. 90, line 39 NOPL. Marriage of François Martin, son of François Martin and Antoinette, to Catherine Montané, daughter of Jean Montané and Mathilda William, 22 July 1875, Our Lady of Sacred Heart, vol. 1, p. 139, AA. Death certificate of Jean Montaneé, Jr., lawful issue of John Montaneé, a native of Africa, with Marie Populus, a native of this city, age one year, died at 232 Prieur Street, 21 April 1876, Recorder of

Births and Deaths, vol. 65, p. 918, microfilm, NOPL.

[76] Death certificate of Jean Montané, age twenty-eight days, died 19 November 1870, Recorder of Births and Deaths, vol. 50, p. 100, microfilm, NOPL.

[77] Succession of John Montaneé, Civil District Court, Parish of Orleans, no. 138844, Division E, Dockett No. 1900, filed 6 October 1921, microfilm, NOPL. The marriage certificate of Jean Montane to Marie Armant is attached in the succession. Hereafter, Montaneé Succession.

[78] Alice Montanet of Bayou Road near Johnson declared Mary Montanet, age five days, died 15 October 1883, Recorder of Deaths, vol. 83, p. 841, NOPL; Oscar Montaneé, age 22, died 17 August 1902, vol. 125, p. 634, NOPL; Joseph Montaneé, age twenty-four, birth place of father, Africa, died 5 July 1900, vol. 133, p. 55, NOPL.

[79] Ibid. n. 76, Montaneé Succession

[80] Ibid. n. 76, Montaneé Succession

[81] Ibid. n. 76 Montaneé Succession

[82] Cemetery Interment Records, St. Roch Cemetery, microfilm, NOPL. Dr. John's wall vault is located on square E, no. 2225, row I, St. Joseph Aisle.

Document 10
Ball of Confusion

This is a reprint of the section of the article focusing on Dr. John Montanee. There is a wealth of information here. The article distills much of use in the preceding nine documents. Madame Trevigne's article is a cornerstone of historical investigations into Dr. John Montanee.

Folklore

Folklore is not so much the word on the street as the word of the street itself about stuff. Ah! The definition is so very inexact and informal that reliability and validity have escaped seeking a more solid ground. We have lost all scientific, all historical credibility. Objectivity has become a kind of excess baggage that can only hold down the flight of memory and rumor. The monochromic dichotomy of true/false has lost itself in a forest inhabited by wildly dancing shades of gray. To paraphrase Heidegger, a true thing is one which presents itself as itself. Fool's gold that presents itself as fool's gold is a "true thing." Folklore that presents itself as folklore is a true thing.

Folklore is a river of information and understandings with tributaries that branch and meander into the very essence of who Dr. John was and is to the people who surround us on the street and are in our lives on a daily basis. This river with its infinite ebbs and flows is best not confused with the historical. Both viewpoints have much to offer to the practitioner. This grimoire's essence is to be found in the voodoo's performance of the three conjures. Rumor, imperfect memory, and mistakes can be as valuable as facts in performing effective conjure.

I will summarize a Tibetan story that nicely illustrates this. Once there was a woman in the mountains living in

very poor circumstances. No food was to be found for her or her children. In desperation she said a mantra she had learned from her mother over a heap of rocks and the rocks turned into a nourishing substance she used to make a soup for her family. She rejoiced and continued saying the mantra and fed her family. After a time, a traveling scholar stopped at her house. She offered him food and told him of her practice with the mantra and stones. He thanked her and added that the mantra was inaccurate; her placement of the words was wrong. She thanked him and, though she now spoke the words correctly, could not again turn the stones into food. Something was missing now. Perhaps it was the very personal, intimate truth that can be found in the expansive soul of folklore, the lore of the folk, our lore which we both preserve and create.

Practitioners have whispered hugely conflicting stories concerning the whereabouts of Marie Laveau's tomb and her rites on Bayou Saint John for many decades. These are secrets to be cherished and closely guarded. Ceremonies at these divergent locations have been both effective and successful. Something that transcends accuracy is working here, maybe something as simple as the strength of the connection between the practitioners and the spirits, buddhas, or loa.

The river of folklore and the information that flows through it is endless. I will include but a bit of flotsam and jetsam most relevant to the work of this grimoire and the practitioner.

Oral Folklore

Some words of the street that I have heard:

Dr. John was a voodoo.
Dr. John was a drummer.
He did calls at rituals while drumming.
He played at rituals on Congo Square.
He knew Marie Laveau and they worked the voodoo together.
He drummed for the rites of Marie Laveau.
He conducted rituals on Congo Square.
He was a Root or Indian Doctor dispensing herbal cures.
He was proud of being able to sign his name.
He is buried in St. Louis No. 1.
He has a strong connection with the spirits of the dead.
Dr. John was a good man.
Dr. John was a bad man.

Written Folklore

VOODOO, PAST, AND PRESENT - Ron Bodin, The Center for Louisiana Studies, University of Southwestern Louisiana. 1990. Ron Bodin is a revered researcher and a personal inspiration.

> "Dr. John – John Montenet, Haitian-born New Orleans Voodoo practitioner who is believed by some to have first integrated traditional Voodoo ways with elements of Catholicism and the snake oracle." (page 94 and 21)

Folkloric elements of this description written in 1990:
- Born in Haiti.
- First to bring Catholicism and Voodoo together.
- First to integrate Voodoo, Catholicism, and the snake oracle.

VOODOO IN NEW ORLEANS - Robert Tallant, Pelican Publishing Company, 1990. This is an excellent resource for the folklore surrounding Dr. John Montanee.

Nathan Barnes (A Black man who had made about 85 years of age), interview in 1944, pages 35 and 36. Concerning a St. John's Eve ceremony. Portions of the interview that have Dr. John playing a drum at one of Marie Laveau's rites are quoted. My comments, largely based on folklore, are in italics.

"He hardly never went to them but I seen him there that night. He was a man about the age I am now and I believes he was kind of broke and low by then."

Dr. John may have attended because he needed money and he could have been paid for playing. He may not have attended earlier ceremonies being relatively wealthy and not needing money till late in his life. Additionally, word is that head male voodoos of that time seldom attended Marie Laveau's rites.

"Marie Laveau was queen then and people say she learned a lot of tricks from old John Bayou *(a name by which Dr. John was known)*. The time I seen him he was still tall and straight and had a white beard. He was leadin' the singin' and beaten' on a barrel covered wit' oxhide wit' two horse's legs. He was old but he was strong and you could hear his voice two miles away. . .I never did forget that. .when I growed up I wanted to be just like old John Bayou."

Pop Abou, a black man in his 80's, speaking about the parties held by Marie Laveau II at the Maison Blanche that he reported attending. (page 86)

"The only music they used was a drum made out of a barrel with a piece of skin stretched over it, and she hired a nigger to beat that with his hands."

Here Marie Laveau II was reported to pay her drummers, at least for more secular events. Marie Laveau II could have acquired this business practice from the original Marie Laveau which would add substance to Dr. John being paid for playing on St. John's Eve.

This has the feel of truth to me. I am always paid for drumming in secular voodoo events and rites, for example media ritual demonstrations. Blessings, weddings, and conformational rites are usually paying. Very seldom do I want pay for works to and for the loa exclusively.

This drum is similar to the one described by Mr. Barnes. The design of the drum is standard and widespread. This does raise the possibility that such a drum was used by Marie Laveau I and II in secular and ritual settings. Two separate informants mention seeing this type of drum.

Tallant also published *The Voodoo Queen* which depicts Dr. John as both a mentor, Dr. John number One, and a rival, Dr. John number Two, of Marie Laveau.

JAMBALAYA: THE NATURAL WOMAN'S BOOK OF PERSONAL CHARMS AND PRACTICAL RITUALS by Luisah Teish, Harper & Row, 1985.

"John Montaigne – also known as Bayou John and Dr. John – was an impressive Senegalese man bearing the tribal marks of a royal family. He had been the slave of a Cuban seaman and had traveled with his master back to

Africa. He purchased his freedom, bought and married fourteen female slaves, and acquired a fifteenth wife, a white woman. This man owned his own home and dressed in elaborate Spanish costumes. Bayou John was widely sought by blacks and whites alike for his herbal remedies and fortune telling.

But the Voudou queens, the women, have always been the true leaders." (page 174)

Luisah Teish is a true Priestess and as such has provided a wonderfully balanced account of Dr. John.

Folkloric elements include Dr. John having been a slave of a Cuban seaman and traveling back to Africa with this seaman. The number of wives cited and his fondness for elaborate Spanish costumes are folkloric.

THE LAST OF THE VOUDOOS by Lafcadio Hearn, Harper's weekly, November 7th, 1885.

In the death of Jean Montanet, at the age of nearly a hundred years, New Orleans lost, at the end of August, the most extraordinary African character that ever gained celebrity within her limits. Jean Montanet, or Jean La Ficelle, or Jean Latanié, or Jean Racine, or Jean Grisgris, or Jean Macaque, or Jean Bayou, or "Voudoo John," or "Bayou John," or "Doctor John" might well have been termed "The Last of the Voudoos"; not that the strange association with which he was affiliated has ceased to exist with his death, but that he was the last really important figure of a long line of wizards or witches whose African titles were recognized, and who exercised an influence over the colored population.

Swarthy occultists will doubtless continue to elect their "queens" and high-priests through years to come, but the influence of the public school is gradually dissipating all faith in witchcraft, and no black hierophant now remains capable of manifesting such mystic knowledge or of inspiring such respect as Voudoo John exhibited and compelled. There will never be another "Rose," another "Marie," much less another Jean Bayou.

It may reasonably be doubted whether any other negro of African birth who lived in the South had a more extraordinary career than that of Jean Montanet. He was a native of Senegal, and claimed to have been a prince's son, in proof of which he was wont to call attention to a number of parallel scars on his cheek, extending in curves from the edge of either temple to the corner of the lips. This fact seems to me partly confirmatory of his statement, as Berenger-Feraud dwells at some length on the fact that the Bambaras, who are probably the finest negro race in Senegal, all wear such disfigurations. The scars are made by gashing the cheeks during infancy, and are considered a sign of race. Three parallel scars mark the freemen of the tribe; four distinguish their captives or slaves. Now Jean's face had, I am told, three scars, which would prove him a free-born Bambara, or at least a member of some free tribe allied to the Bambaras, and living upon their territory. At all events, Jean possessed physical characteristics answering to those by which the French ethnologists in Senegal distinguish the Bambaras. He was of middle height, very strongly built, with broad shoulders, well-developed muscles, an inky black skin, retreating forehead, small bright eyes, a very flat nose, and a woolly beard, gray only during the last few years

of his long life. He had a resonant voice and a very authoritative manner.

At an early age he was kidnapped by Spanish slavers, who sold him at some Spanish port, whence he was ultimately shipped to Cuba. His West-Indian master taught him to be an excellent cook, ultimately became attached to him, and made him a present of his freedom. Jean soon afterward engaged on some Spanish vessel as ship's cook, and in the exercise of this calling voyaged considerably in both hemispheres. Finally tiring of the sea, he left his ship at New Orleans, and began life on shore as a cotton-roller. His physical strength gave him considerable advantage above his fellow-blacks; and his employers also discovered that he wielded some peculiar occult influence over the negroes, which made him valuable as an overseer or gang leader. Jean, in short, possessed the mysterious obi power, the existence of which has been recognized in most slave-holding communities, and with which many a West-Indian planter has been compelled by force of circumstances to effect a compromise. Accordingly Jean was permitted many liberties which other blacks, although free, would never have presumed to take. Soon it became rumored that he was a seer of no small powers, and that he could tell the future by the marks upon bales of cotton. I have never been able to learn the details of this queer method of telling fortunes; but Jean became so successful in the exercise of it that thousands of colored people flocked to him for predictions and counsel, and even white people, moved by curiosity or by doubt, paid him to prophesy for them. Finally he became wealthy enough to abandon the levee and purchase a large tract of property on the

Bayou Road, where he built a house. His land extended from Prieur Street on the Bayou Road as far as Roman, covering the greater portion of an extensive square, now well built up. In those days it was a marshy green plain, with a few scattered habitations.

At his new home Jean continued the practice of fortune-telling, but combined it with the profession of creole medicine, and of arts still more mysterious. By-and-by his reputation became so great that he was able to demand and obtain immense fees. People of both races and both sexes thronged to see him—many coming even from far-away creole towns in the parishes, and well-dressed women, closely veiled, often knocked at his door. Parties paid from ten to twenty dollars for advice, for herb medicines, for recipes to make the hair grow, for cataplasms supposed to possess mysterious virtues, but really made with scraps of shoe-leather triturated into paste, for advice what ticket to buy in the Havana Lottery, for aid to recover stolen goods, for love powers, for counsel in family troubles, for charms by which to obtain revenge upon an enemy. Once Jean received a fee of fifty dollars for a potion. "It was water," he said to a creole confidant, "with some common herbs boiled in it. I hurt nobody; but if folks want to give me fifty dollars, I take the fifty dollars every time!" His office furniture consisted of a table, a chair, a picture of the Virgin Mary, an elephant's tusk, some shells which he said were African shells and enabled him to read the future, and a pack of cards in each of which a small hole had been burned. About his person he always carried two small bones wrapped around with a black string, which bones he really appeared to revere as fetiches.

Wax candles were burned during his performances; and as he bought a whole box of them every few days during "flush times," one can imagine how large the number of his clients must have been. They poured money into his hands so generously that he became worth at least $50,000!

Then, indeed, did this possible son of a Bambara prince begin to live more grandly than any black potentate of Senegal. He had his carriage and pair, worthy of a planter, and his blooded saddle-horse, which he rode well, attired in a gaudy Spanish costume, and seated upon an elaborately decorated Mexican saddle. At home, where he ate and drank only the best--scorning claret worth less than a dollar the *litre*—he continued to find his simple furniture good enough for him; but he had at least fifteen wives—a harem worthy of Boubakar-Segou. White folks might have called them by a less honorific name, but Jean declared them his legitimate spouses according to African ritual. One of the curious features in modern slavery was the ownership of blacks by freedmen of their own color, and these negro slave-holders were usually savage and merciless masters. Jean was not; but it was by right of slave purchase that he obtained most of his wives, who bore him children in great multitude. Finally he managed to woo and win a white woman of the lowest class, who might have been, after a fashion, the Sultana-Validé of this Seraglio. On grand occasions Jean used to distribute largess among the colored population of his neighborhood in the shape of food—bowls of *gombo* or dishes of *jimbalaya*. He did it for popularity's sake in those days, perhaps; but in after-years, during the great epidemics, he did it for charity,

even when so much reduced in circumstances that he was himself obliged to cook the food to be given away.

But Jean's greatness did not fail to entail certain cares. He did not know what to do with his money. He had no faith in banks, and had seen too much of the darker side of life to have much faith in human nature. For many years he kept his money under-ground, burying or taking it up at night only, occasionally concealing large sums so well that he could never find them again himself; and now, after many years, people still believe there are treasures entombed somewhere in the neighborhood of Prieur Street and Bayou Road. All business negotiations of a serious character caused him much worry, and as he found many willing to take advantage of his ignorance, he probably felt small remorse for certain questionable actions of his own. He was notoriously bad pay, and part of his property was seized at last to cover a debt. Then, in an evil hour, he asked a man without scruples to teach him how to write, believing that financial misfortunes were mostly due to ignorance of the alphabet. After he had learned to write his name, he was innocent enough one day to place his signature by request at the bottom of a blank sheet of paper, and, lo! his real estate passed from his possession in some horribly mysterious way. Still he had some money left, and made heroic efforts to retrieve his fortunes. He bought other property, and he invested desperately in lottery tickets. The lottery craze finally came upon him, and had far more to do with his ultimate ruin than his losses in the grocery, the shoemaker's shop, and other establishments into which he had put several thousand dollars as the silent partner of people who cheated him. He might certainly have

continued to make a good living, since people still sent for him to cure them with his herbs, or went to see him to have their fortunes told; but all his earnings were wasted in tempting fortune. After a score of seizures and a long succession of evictions, he was at last obliged to seek hospitality from some of his numerous children; and of all he had once owned nothing remained to him but his African shells, his elephant's tusk, and the sewing-machine table that had served him to tell fortunes and to burn wax candles upon. Even these, I think, were attached a day or two before his death, which occurred at the house of his daughter by the white wife, an intelligent mulatto with many children of her own.

Jean's ideas of religion were primitive in the extreme. The conversion of the chief tribes of Senegal to Islam occurred in recent years, and it is probable that at the time he was captured by slavers his people were still in a condition little above gross fetichism. If during his years of servitude in a Catholic colony he had imbibed some notions of Romish Christianity, it is certain at least that the Christian ideas were always subordinated to the African—just as the image of the Virgin Mary was used by him merely as an auxiliary fetich in his witchcraft, and was considered as possessing much less power than the "elephant's toof." He was in many respects a humbug; but he may have sincerely believed in the efficacy of certain superstitious rites of his own. He stated that he had a Master whom he was bound to obey; that he could read the will of this Master in the twinkling of the stars; and often of clear nights the neighbors used to watch him standing alone at some street corner staring at the welkin, pulling his woolly beard, and talking in an

unknown language to some imaginary being. Whenever Jean indulged in this freak, people knew that he needed money badly, and would probably try to borrow a dollar or two from some one in the vicinity next day.

Testimony to his remarkable skill in the use of herbs could be gathered from nearly every one now living who became well acquainted with him. During the epidemic of 1878, which uprooted the old belief in the total immunity of negroes and colored people from yellow fever, two of Jean's children were "taken down." "I have no money," he said, "but I can cure my children," which he proceeded to do with the aid of some weeds plucked from the edge of the Prieur Street gutters. One of the herbs, I am told, was what our creoles call the "parasol." "The children were playing on the banquette next day," said my informant.

Montanet, even in the most unlucky part of his career, retained the superstitious reverence of colored people in all parts of the city. When he made his appearance even on the American side of Canal Street to doctor some sick person, there was always much subdued excitement among the colored folks, who whispered and stared a great deal, but were careful not to raise their voices when they said, "Dar's Hoodoo John!" That an unlettered African slave should have been able to achieve what Jean Bayou achieved in a civilized city, and to earn the wealth and the reputation that he enjoyed during many years of his life, might be cited as a singular evidence of modern popular credulity, but it is also proof that Jean was not an ordinary man in point of natural intelligence.

This definitive article considered by many as Dr. John's

functional obituary is a chronicling of his life and a gumbo of historical fact and folkloric understandings. In order to separate the two, it is best read in the light of Barbara Trevigne's and Carolyn Morrow Long's research.

THE FRENCH QUARTER by Herbert Asbury, Pocket Books, 1949 (first published by Alfed Knoph, 1936)

> "The first Voodoo doctor of whom there is any record in New Orleans was a huge coal-black negro with a tattooed face, who called himself Dr. John, and who flourished during the early and middle 1840's. He was a mind-reader and a dabbler in astrology. ."(page 191)

The passage continues and associates Dr. John with Pauline, through a love-philter she purchased from him. Pauline was an enslaved mulatto who was the first person of color to be executed under the Black Code under the American occupation in 1846. Dr. John was also described by the author as retiring with a fortune. (page 192)

THE SPIRITUAL CHURCHES OF NEW ORLEANS: Origins, Beliefs, and Rituals of an African-American Religion by Claude F. Jacobs and Andrew J. Kaslow, University of Tennessee Press, 1991

> ". .Dr. John was one of New Orleans' most famous Voodoos, who allegedly conducted rites with Marie Laveau on Bayou St. John on June 23rd, St. John's Eve." (page 91)

> "Leafy Anderson had among her spirit guides a 'great doctor and minister,' Doctor John, whose power

was supposed to equal that of St. Jude, the 'saint of impossible cases'." (page 149)

"Leafy Anderson said Father John was a great doctor and a great minister." (interview with church members, page 134)

"Since some aspects of the churches' belief and ritual are traceable to Louisiana Voodoo, Father John may be Dr. John, one of the most famous mid-nineteenth–century practitioners of the Afro-Catholic syncretic cult." (page 135)

Leafy Anderson was the founder of the Spiritual Church Movement in New Orleans, Louisiana in the 1920s. The authors do point out that an alternate origin of Father John may be a popular patent medicine of the day, "Father John's." (page 135)

NEW ORLEANS VOODOO TAROT by Louis Martinié and Sallie Ann Glassman, Destiny Books, 1992

"Dr. John is a New Orleans personage who is traveling the starry road to the position of loa. He was a practitioner and sacred drummer of high renown. .(his) face was said to be tattooed with red and blue lines in the form of snakes. .The Spirit of the first Dr. John resides close to Congo Square in St. Louis Cemetery No. 1. Dr. John is a great patron of ritual drummers." (Twenty-Two Roads/ Major Arcana; Road Number 1, Dr. John/The Magus. (pages 38 and 39)

> "Dr. John – A Voodoo practitioner and drummer in New Orleans during the beginning of the nineteenth century." (Glossary, page 261)

I relied heavily on folklore as a source in writing these quoted lines, the word on the street from practitioners, and the work of Mr. Tallant. There was very little substantive historical research focused on Dr. John a quarter century ago. I am very pleased that his path to loa is coming to fruition. As an aside, upon looking back into the tarot I realized that the first quote in the book is from Aleister Crowley and the closely following second quote from Ernie K-Doh. Ah! Quite a pairing, if only they could have met.

DR. JOHN (Malcolm John "Mac" Rebennack, the present Dr. John; The Wikipedia, an electric encyclopedia).

> "I actually got a clipping from the Times Picayune newspaper about how my great-great-great-grandpa Wayne was busted with this guy for runnin' a voodoo operation in a whorehouse in 1860. I decided I would produce the record with this as a concept."

This can be compared to Document #3 in the Historical section of this book. In 1850 John Montanet was listed with a "Profession, Occupation, Trade…" of "Coffeehouse." Coffeehouse has enjoyed past use as a genteel term for whorehouse.

A PRIEST'S HEAD, A DRUMMER'S HANDS by Louis Martinié, Black Moon Publishing, 2010. A New Orleans Voodoo Heritage Edition.

The following text and photo-graphs are excerpted from A Priest's Head, A Drummer's Hands, pages 105 to 109, 116.

They describe the encounter Mishlen Linden and I had that identified the folkloric burial place of Dr. John at St. Louis Cemetery No. 1 in an isle behind the tomb of Marie Laveau. I am quite sure that this is where a portion of his spirit resides. Linda Falorio's painting of the tomb of Dr. John is a sure path that can be followed to his presence.

The First Dr. John of New Orleans Voodoo

There are the loa who have found their origin in the thick ethers of New Orleans history. They, and the rites performed to honor them, form the living heart of New Orleans Voodoo. Our Voodoo Doctors are central to the beat of this heart.

Dr. John may well stand as primary in the line of known New Orleans Voodoo Doctors. Many of the loa began as men and women who walked the rather straightforward paths of the Visible World. The rich mix of time and their deeds moved these men and women into the more malleable regions of memory, then folklore, then legend, and finally myth. All of these provinces overlap, their boundaries do not so much contain as breathe life into the flora and fauna of adjacent regions. The perfumes of these provinces mix and swirl and create and destroy. The past is as malleable as our memories. The roads we walk are paved with the memories we choose to remember as persons, as communities, and as a people.

Osiris lies in pieces. This is one re-membering. One face of spirit.

Littany to the Good Doctor

Doctor John

Honor and respect to you.

I remember your name.

I say your name.

Before my eyes sits the issue of your hand; in both document and signature.

Within me my mind and heart remember you.

Doctor John

Jean Montanée.

Born of Africa

Lived in New Orleans.

Husband to Mathilde and Armantine

Father of John Montannet born the third of November, 1856

And of many others.

Owner of a coffeehouse in New Orleans.

Worked as physician and Indian Doctor.

Passed on August 18, 1885 at 70 years.

Doctor John

Loa of New Orleans.

Loa of Drummers.

Loa of Doctors in the Spiritual Path.

Guide my hands on this drum

Guide my hands in this Work.

Doctor John

Speak in wisdom to my mind

Speak in understanding to my heart.

Help me to play the rhythms of awakening to my Spirit.

Touch and be Touched.

The Tomb of Dr. John, All Saints Day, 2009

The Tomb of Dr. John by Linda Falorio

A Talisman For Dr. John

The black man walking toward Mishlen and I had remarkably blue eyes. The age that rode upon him also left its imprint on his semi-formal, black clothing. He was dusty, as if he had been sleeping in the cemetery.

The three of us talked. He said the kids might come up with a gun, that they were so poor and to just give them money if they wanted it. He kept asking if Mishlen was black or white. It was obvious that he walked a road much wider than the Visible. I felt, and can still feel, the strength of his spirit. I asked if I could give him any money for his time and he declined. The man showed us the tomb of the original Dr. John. (circa 1989)

The photo on the previous page is that of the tomb taken on All Saints Day 2009 with the document signed by Dr. John on one ledge. His signature was annointed with red palm oil and white coconut oil. We had just finished a public rite to Marie Laveau and I was with the Misfits' drummer, they were playing at Voodoo Fest, a large popular music festival in New Orleans. I played to Dr. John and we both asked him to strengthen the voice of our drums. The drummer then left a drum key he had used for decades on the tomb.

The historical document (appearing on pages 41-45 of this Grimoire), signed by the first Dr. John, is presented as a talisman. It speaks of age, worth, and accomplishment. As any talisman, it can be used as a bridge. Invite what is of value to yourself and to your community.

Present Photographs of The Tombs of Dr. John in St. Louis No. 1 and of St. Roch Cemetery

The two tombs of Dr. John are a fine example of the Historic (Saint Roch Cemetery) and the Folkloric (St. Louis No. 1) points of view. Both are of use to the voodoos in their conjures. Both contain the real tomb of Dr. John.

St. Louis No. 1, Folkloric Tomb of Dr. John

Additional photos of St. Louis No. 1 Cemetery

St. Roch Cemetery, Historical Grave site of Dr. John.

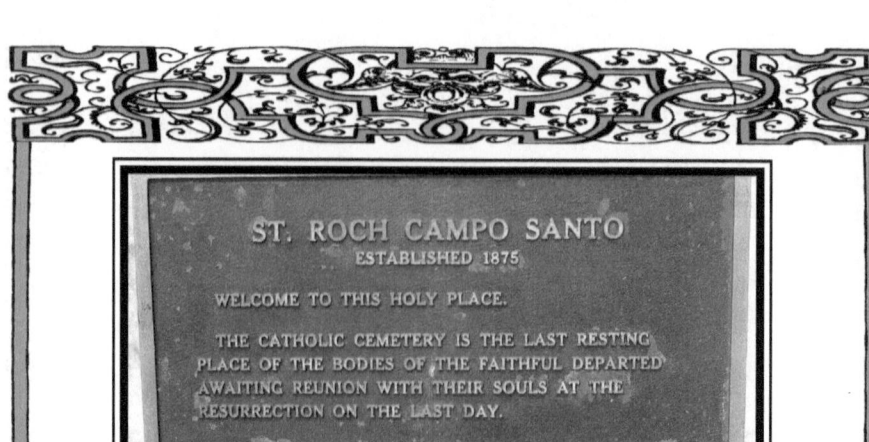

Additional photos of St. Roch Cemetery

Voices of the Community
Experiments, Explorations, Experiences, Investigations, Teachings, and Conjures

The offerings to and conjures/contacts with Dr. John Montanee are ongoing. We are building this body of information, knowledge, understanding, and wisdom together. Experimentation, exploration, and communication are the keystones of our conjures.

The conjures offered to Dr. John Montanee will surely move from a trickle, to a stream, to a river flowing between the Visible and Invisible Worlds carrying the power and grace so necessary for manifestation. Dr. John, if his resurrection is to bear its greatest possible value, must be equally available to the entire community. Dr. John is his own man and will direct his attention according to his own will.

If contact with the Good Doctor is presented or understood as restricted to an in some way privileged segment of the community, then the river of conjures and offerings is choked and service to his becoming will be as constrained as is the natural flow of the Mississippi. Dr. John will break out, as does the mighty Mississippi with

its floods and topped levees. Why invite such tedious and repetitive destruction, especially after the Storm (Hurricane Katrina), when it is not necessary?

It is my hope that portions of the explorations and experiments contradict one another. It is so easy to fall into the reductionist trap of "one true interpretation." This is the small arena of the One True God and the infallible words of His great profits, be they power over others or money. This can be particularly insidious in the case of our explorations and experiments when the information flows from a direct contact with Dr. John Montanee. Direct revelation is as open to question as any other way of knowing. Perhaps "He said..." is better phrased as "He told me..." or "I was told he spoke through me and said..." The "me" in the statements is an important step back from infallible revelation.

The Visible and Invisible Universes in which we live are both closer and further apart than we can ever imagine. They require room to express themselves in the fullness of their being, a fullness that nurtures a completeness containing elements that often appear contradictory. It would be a pity to allow our, at times, limited understandings to act as a filter to such an awe full completeness. Restriction is a feeble substitute for the splendor of these universes as they expand beyond the very concept of "limit."

Notes, Records, and Documents

I have included only a small sample of the present explorations, experiments, and conjures. Also, at this point of our working, I believe it is opportune to include records of sessions introducing individuals and groups to the

knowledge we have pertaining to Dr. John.

DrJohnVoodoo.com is sponsored by Black Moon Publishing and is a nexus dedicated to making all of our ongoing experiments, explorations, experiences, investigations, teachings, and conjures available to practitioners. The material in this section will be available on the Dr. John Voodoo website. In addition the documents in the historical section will be available for download on the website as high definition jpeg files.

To contribute to this Working please contact us at drjohn@drjohnvoodoo.com with the name you wish to use, and the date and location of the experience if applicable. Writings of any length, one sentence to book length, are both proper and important. Together we will re-member Dr. John Montanee much as Osiris was re-membered.

Voices of the Community
Festival Teachings, Conjures, and Magickal Records

Dr. Louie Martinié

Gryphon's Nest Festivals, Louisiana

Magickal Record: 2010

I brought present day Dr. John's Prayer to stop the oil to give to festival participants. A few months ago I was doing a drum prayer for clear waters at the New Orleans Voodoo Spiritual Temple. Dr. John (Mac Rebennack) called the Temple and dictated a beautiful prayer he got from Spirit for protection of the waters. Norma, who works at the Temple, brought the prayer in and I played with it on the head of my drum. Very powerful.

Prayer by Dr. John (5.6.2010)
Recite at Sundown

Great Spirit, Mother God, Father God
Surround your people with white light
To protect them from harm.
Send your spirit guides to keep the earth strong;
Angels to protect the land from the oil;
The waters from pollution;
The animals from the storm.
Surround us with your holy light,
Smile upon us to keep us strong,
Preserve the land.

Spare your children and enlighten the masses.
Give us a solution.
Four winds blow; swirl to the sea.
While the white light shines and
protects the sacred center.
Remove the earth from the path of harm.
Forgive the transgressors.
Let the light remove the dark.

DR. JOHN (JOHN MONTANEE): DRUM SESSION AND BLESSING, 2011

Rhythms from The New Orleans Voodoo Spiritual Temple will serve as the basis for improvisation in the drum session. Participants, who wish, will be given the opportunity to use copies of the signature of John Montanee to bring his blessing into their drum.

DR. JOHN (JOHN MONTANEE): WHAT IS KNOWN, 2011

The session will consist of a discussion centering on the original Dr. John (John Montanee) and his position in New Orleans Voodoo. New historical documents, research, and folklore will be presented dating from the rituals on Congo Square in the eighteen hundreds.

MAGICKAL RECORD: 2012

I brought the Dr. John historical documents to Gryphon's Nest festival to share with other participants and presenters. Before drumming for a Wiccan Rite during the event, I passed out copies of Dr. John's signature to the drummers during this Festival.

Starwood Festivals

Magickal Record: Upstate New York, 2002

Drummers gave a "thank you" to Carolyn Long for finding the signature of Dr. John Montanee. A paper thanking Carolyn Long was passed around at the festival and later at the New Orleans Voodoo Spiritual Temple and signed by beaucoup drummers.

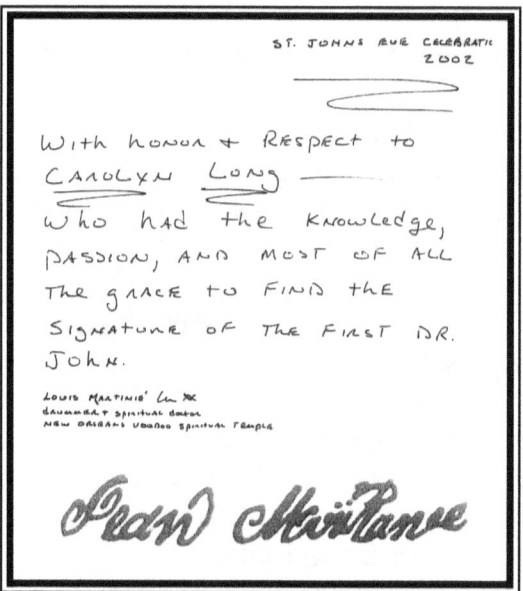

(*This is a copy of the note the drummers signed that helped to inspire Carolyn Long to continue her intense research into Dr. John Montanee.*)

Magickal Record: 2010

This is the year of the BP oil spill in the Gulf of Mexico. We drove through oily rain on the coast by Pensacola, Florida. I stopped at a gas station to clean the windshield

on our automobile and asked the attendant about the rain. He just said, "Yeah, don't worry. It'll stop when they plug the well."

New Orleans Voodoo, An Order of Service: Upstate New York, 2010

During this ritual session drum prayers and rhythms developed at ceremonies held between 1995 and 2000 by the New Orleans Voodoo Spiritual Temple will be taught. These prayers/rhythms are part of a unique Order of Service based upon birthing. These rhythms are played with the head, heart, and hands. The session will end with an honor bound confirmation in this Order of Service given through the loa blanc dan-i. The prayers and rhythms can be learnt without participating in the confirmation. Emphasis in the session will be on paying honor and respect to Dr. John Montanee. Dr. John Montanee played with Marie Laveau on Congo Square and is a major loa in the line of New Orleans Voodoo Drummers and Doctors.

Prayer and Conjure to Stop The Oil!!!: Upstate New York, 2010
(See Gryphon's Nest Festivals, Magickal Record, 2010, page 118 for the text of the prayer and the background of its reception.)

At this Starwood rite, we will pass out copies of the prayer with a veve drawn on the back using oil less waters from the Mississippi. A pure white feather from the wetlands (We live next to Saint Bernard Parish) will be used to clean the head of each drum before playing. It would be good for each of us to recite the prayer while playing with the prayer on the drum head. A tasty calinda rhythm will be taught and played. The copies of the drum prayer are from

Maegdlyn and the feathers are from Mishlen Linden.

This is something we are all doing together. We are all spiritual warriors. It makes sense to use the power that we have to protect the beauty and lives around us for ourselves and others. A discussion of the oil will follow the prayer.

MAGICKAL RECORD: 2010

A number of practitioners brought oil from the spill to the Starwood Festival. The oil was used in the prayer/conjure as a link to the spill. We rubbed the oil on our hands and then cleaned the oil off. No one knows if the well can be capped. There are globs of oil on the beaches and the shrimps and birds.

DR. JOHN MONTANEE, DRUM LOA: WEST VIRGINIA, 2012

Dr. John Montanee was one of the first and perhaps the most powerful of the early Voodoo Drummers and Doctors (approx. 1815 to 1885). An historical and a folkloric discussion of Dr. John's life will be provided. This will be followed by a rite in which dust and waters from the Doctor's gravesite will be combined with his signature and documents from his life to invite this grand loa to enter the hands and drum heads of the ritualists.

NEW ORLEANS VOODOO; AN ORDER OF SERVICE: WEST VIRGINIA, 2012

During this ritual session drum prayers and rhythms developed at ceremonies held between 1995 and 2000 by the New Orleans Voodoo Spiritual Temple will be taught. . as per Order of Service above. . Dr. John Montanee played with Marie Laveau on Congo Square and is a major loa in the line of New Orleans Voodoo Drummers and Doctors.

Notes From Magickal Record: West Virginia, 2012

• I left DJ signatures out last night and we got a lot of rain, it was torrential so he got a lot of water. Water is a favored offering.

• Stand tall. .Dr. John. .stand tall and in that darkness look for signs. Stand tall and look for signs in that darkness. . the darkness is the emerald tablet. .that is the sky, that is the sky upon which I will write.

• Ritual; Dr. John Air. .looking into the sky, looking for signs in the stars and in the dark places between the stars and in the day sky.

• From a woman attending the rite and making automatic drawings:

"When I did it I didn't look at it. And the first time I looked at it first thing I saw was I thought I saw a face, you know I see the hair. .and I see a strong jaw. .it is a really strong face. But then you look at it again and there is a path. .if you look here it's the crossroads. And there is a lot of depth to it. .I remember when I did it. .I did it the whole time that the ceremony went on. .I put my pen down. .it was automatic. .this is something they did in the 1920s. .it was afraid. .but I figured what the heck. .what I felt through the pen is that there are places where it glided and where it was slippery."

• Badal Roy. . stopped by and said his name means rain. . it was raining when he was born, his father pointed to the sky and they named him. (DJ and the importance of water in his conjures; see records from Babalon conjures.)

• In the dome looking up at the night sky. .Sallie's drawing of the gesture "as above so below" with the Dr. John (Magus) card in the New Orleans Voodoo Tarot. Sallie's art mirrors and foretells Dr. John looking to the

sky for signs.
- Magickal Practice: Keeping my eyes half closed and in so doing the top part is the night sky. Dr. John looked to the night sky
- The tops of the trees around Caffinas Coffee House outline the sky creating an immense vessica. That is the sky upon which I will write. That is the sky upon which I will write. .I just closed my eyes and in the darkness and I saw Dr. John Montanee's name (signature). That is the sky upon which I will write.

BABALON RISING FESTIVALS

DR. JOHN MONTANEE: PATRON OF RITUAL DRUMMERS TO DRUM LOA, INDIANA 2012

Dr. John Montanee was one of the first and perhaps the most powerful of the early New Orleans Voodoo Drummers and Doctors (approx. 1815 to 1885). An historical and a folkloric discussion of Dr. John's life will be provided. The position of Dr. John as the Magus in the *New Orleans Voodoo Tarot* (Martinié and Glassman, 1992) and New Orleans Voodoo in general will be discussed. This will be followed by a description of a rite in which dust and waters from the Doctor's gravesite will be combined with his signatures and documents from his life to invite this great spirit to enter the head, heart, hands, and drum heads of the ritualists.

FRIDAY RITUAL TO DR. JOHN MONTANEE: NEW ORLEANS DRUM PATRON TO LOA, INDIANA 2012

(This was a more formal rite/conjure scheduled by the Festival.)

An altar to Dr. John Montanee will be constructed and

those attending will be invited to leave gifts. Dust and waters from the Doctor's gravesite will be combined with his signatures and documents from his life and used to invite this grand loa to enter the head, heart, and hands of the drummers and their drum's heads. This ritual is meant to offer honor and respect to the good Doctor; to invite him to rejoin the community of living drummers, not to ask anything of him. It is a celebration of Dr. John's transition from "patron of ritual drummers (*New Orleans Voodoo Tarot*; Martinié and Glassman, 1992)" to drum loa. Attendance at an earlier session is helpful in the performance of this ritual though not necessary. Please bring any percussion instruments you may have. Dancers are very welcome.

Notes From Magickal Record: Friday Night Conjure/Ritual, Indiana, 2012

In this ritual we are asking for no particular thing so every particular thing is possible. What we are giving is a gift or a present. No strings attached, we are not going fishing. The rite is more like a welcome party or a house warming, the houses being us.

These are some of the ways DJ can enter us. Head (thoughts) - He can manifest in thought. Heart (blood-emotions) - He can manifest in emotions. Hands (technique – motor memory) - He can manifest in motor/movement. All of these taken together generally describe classic possession or being taken by spirit.

Drum Head –The drum is an altar to a Temple Drummer (and a Mardi Gras Indian). As such, it is receptive to subtle fluctuations in grace.

DESCRIPTION OF THE CONJURE/RITUAL:

Construction: A maypole functions as the center post. There is an altar in middle of a circle. The altar consists of 5 drums –earth/air/fire/water/spirit. The drums are laid out in the shape of a crossroads as a veve. Materials on these 5 drums consist of waters from St. Roch's Cemetery, graveyard dust from St. Roch, red palm oil, and coconut oil. Items consist of a frock coat, fire, and the Doctor's signature.

Order of Service of the Conjure/Ritual: Marassa (Mamie Waters rhythm) then Morts (Mamie Waters rhythm) then Mysteries (Legba's rhythm with Callings). Then begin Bamboula rhythm; the Bamboula can change to other rhythms as the loa come. Voodoos come up to the altar (drums) in any order. I am with the Doctor's signature in the center of the crossroads. Earth is used with the Doctor's signature to open the voodoos that come to the center. Then they go back and drum, dance, or actively listen. Gifts or presents to the Doctor can be left at any time. After all come up, we continue to drum, dance, or listen.

End the rite with the 5 drums being moved to touch one another in the center. Sprinkle area and voodoos with Florida Water. Continue to drum and dance; contact with Dr. John and the level of the contact is an individual choice.

We are all witnesses to see and remember what comes of our actions so that the rites can grow by accretion. This can lead to an unfolding of the aspects and the attributes of Dr. John Montanee.

I am very open to discuss any experiences after the

conjure/rite.

Priest Oswan Chamani taught that it is disrespectful to make too many plans. I remember him throwing a chair down the stairs to the first Temple at someone who insisted that he "practice" a rite.

SOME OBSERVATIONS:

• A woman (medical) was very thirsty even though she hydrated all day. She said she must have drunk a half gallon of the Doctor's water from St. Roch's Cemetery. She was laughing and crying, this was first time for her to be taken by spirit in this manner.

• A woman brought 2 feathers, she took a bowl of water with graveyard earth and water around to the voodoos. This was very effective.

• When I was taking the Saint Roch earth out of the container I saw a caterpillar grub and as I held it there was movement. This emissary of the insect loa has traveled quite a long way. It squirmed between my first 2 fingers on my right hand and began to painfully borrow into my hand. I took it to a clump of grass on the side and shook it to the earth telling the grub to tell its grandfather and grandmother I saved it. This underground life form is now in the earth by the ritual space in Babalon, Our Haven, Indiana.

NOTES FROM MAGICKAL RECORD, THURSDAY RITUAL TO DR. JOHN MONTANEE: INDIANA, 2012

This conjure was less formal, unscheduled. It took place in a back circle well off of the festival field.

• Phil Farber and Maegdlyn performed an NLP exercise immediately before the rite.

• A large man in a kilt fell to the ground, coughing. He

was down for most of rite, Marty was with him.

• I could feel (sense of calm, lightness in the chest area) Maegdlyn balancing me in the rite. My level of confidence in this less formal ceremony went up. I had felt that something was missing in me, there was an edge of unsureness. I became more assured as the rite developed; we will work and bring the Doctor presents and gifts of exactly what we have. We begin where we are. Now I more fully realize one reason why Priestess Miriam values my presence at rites. She says that I balance her.

• Phil Farber said he was drawn to look up at the stars, one star was changing color. There were bright spots combining individual stars in the sky. He thought that this sky gazing may be a distraction from the rite. At the conclusion of the rite, I said that Dr. John would look to the sky for messages. Phil was surprised. Folklore has DJ looking to the sky for messages. These messages could have been connected to astrology and/or direct communications from what the Doctor saw in the sky.

• A man saw a cat with the face of something like a goat; the lines of the face were hard edged.

• Don Kraig felt a constriction around his neck. He heard, "The Doctor will teach the voodoo to his children, he will teach the inner voodoo to his child Louie." Two numbers came up possibly 4 and 7. Don saw the Doctor sitting on a high seat. He heard him say to sit tall, stand tall. He saw that he cuts off both ends of a cigar then smokes both parts.

• Neal, standing on the side lines for some time, could feel the love.

• Three? men and women found it hard to breathe.

• There was much coughing in the rite. People were going down, taken by spirit.

Voices of the Community
Experiments, Explorations, Experiences, and Conjures
Always Listen to the Doctor

© 2014 Claudia Williams

I constantly marvel at it: How the energy of a person one may never have met or have an opportunity to meet can still alter your life. The man who remains today New Orleans' premier male Vodou practitioner, Dr. John and his remaining energy here played a major role in altering my life path. I am eternally grateful.

My husband and I first visited New Orleans in 1991. We were occultists, but not terribly familiar with Vodou. We ventured into the New Orleans Voodoo Museum one miserably hot August afternoon and were greeted by one of the most gorgeous women I'd ever seen, a Voodoo priestess named Margaret, who I came to know, admire and have the privilege to call friend. She took us on a tour of the museum. Her spirit and spirituality were palpable. She oozed truth, beauty, charm and power.

The items in the museum were/are spectacular. (We continue to build our own occult museum now with theirs as inspiration.) On a chair there sat an old, slightly tattered top hat. Margaret saw I was immediately mesmerized, "It belonged to the great Voodoo man, Doctor John" she smiled. To me, the hat was alive, glowing with the essence of the man who'd owned and worn it. I could see the power of the man, I could sense his own feeling of pride when he donned that hat and went to work helping people with his

skills. The worn black satin glowed with a life force still imbued in it by its owner.

As we left that day, Margaret pointed to my pentacle necklace and said, "We learn from each other." Over the next three years I visited the museum several times. A year after the first visit I was delighted when I walked in and Margaret remembered me. Right away I was ushered in to visit the hat. Still it glowed. Still it spoke to me. A little louder with each visit, "You belong HERE now. THIS is the work you should be doing."

Our last visit before purchasing our home and moving here, we stayed in an apartment behind the museum. One day, the late Charles Gandolfo, an owner of the museum, took us on another tour. I think he'd heard about the girl with the hat fascination. He picked it up and inspected it for a moment, "I don't let people touch these things as a rule," he said, "but in this case I think it's all right." He held out the hat for me to hold. I held it as best I could to show reverence and appreciation for the special privilege.

I saw the magnificent specter of Dr. John in my mind's eye. "You're almost here," I heard him say. "You'll know when the Spirits call you and you will come to us and bring your own abilities to share." In fact we were in the process of purchasing our home and moving from New York City to New Orleans. I was doing psychic work professionally, though not yet working with the Orisha or Loa. Without missing a beat, Charles took back the hat, saying, "He's talkative today." He inspected the hat as if to make sure he didn't miss any messages intended for him. Looking slightly disappointed, he returned the top hat to its place.

I thought of these marvelous people I had met; Margaret, Charles and others. THAT is what I want, what I aspire

to, I thought. I hope to leave a legacy of energy and inspiration. To think someday someone might hold an item that had been mine and walk away feeling a positive change for having touched upon that spirit, that energy. I felt a sense of healing and renewal that was extraordinary. I will remember those visits with Dr. John's hat always. As my personal spiritual practice has for many years now been in the West African based traditions, the energy I communed with was correct, this was where I belonged.

I know to always listen to the Doctor.

DR. JOHN MONTANEE: THE PHYSICIAN'S MESSAGE IS KNOW THYSELF

© 2014 Lilith Dorsey

As legends of New Orleans go, Dr. John Montanee is the original. There is more legend than fact surrounding this larger than life character. Many, myself included, view him as one of New Orleans' Voodoo's earliest drummers whose rhythms beat in our blood, in our memory, in our subconscious. There is not a ritual in or about New Orleans that does not flow forth from this forefather.

Legend has it that he was from Senegal, and it came to me the other night that he was the first "lost boy" the leader, the progenitor of what they could and would find in a world very different from their home. Recent history has seen a mass exodus from that country, and many of the struggles the displaced "lost boys" have found here regarding money and mentality are not unlike those demons that chased Dr. John. The inspiration he left behind is that

he was a true doctor healing people on the deepest levels with divination and magick. He came to the U.S. from a land very different, but he made the necessary changes to survive and thrive doing whatever he could.

His message, as my Voodoo Priestess ears hear and understand it, is a Gede message, a message from the dead, "you take yourself with you, so you damn well better know your self." We all create ourselves, and I can only imagine who Dr. John Montanee set out to be when he arrived on this planet hundreds of years ago. Transported to New Orleans he took on a new identity, and urban legend has layered on even more shades of meaning surrounding this man who was very much a magickal mystery. Fact has fucked fiction and the babe is beautiful.

Dr. John Montanee's Ashe (sacred energy), rhythms, and movements when I have witnessed them are tribal and transformative. I have experienced dozens of rituals where we were blessed with the benefit of Dr. John Montanee's Ashe. These ceremonies have been everywhere from the banks of the Mississippi with Priestess Miriam Chamani, to the large stage with Mac Rebennack (the world famous Jazz legend, Dr. John), to the Bayou St. John with my dearly departed friend Cayne, to the wild and wonderful Starwood festivals with Louis Martinié, as well as with my own amazing godchildren in my spiritual home. I have always felt his power as protective and unifying. He embraces with heartiness and love those who come to him with respect and honor. Dr. John Montanee is capable of infinite wisdom and limitless capacity, assuming you understand the perimeters. That statement isn't a paradoxical caveat, it's a doorway. Open it wisely.

Gris Gris Lamp for Doctor John Montanee

© 2014 Denise Alvarado

Doctor John Montanee is the Father of New Orleans Voudou, the loa of drummers and rootdoctors, and patron to male Voudou practitioners and female rootwomen.

This magic gris gris lamp was given to me by Doctor John in a dream along with a box of other mysteries. It was a typical sweltering hot day and I was sitting on my front porch in the French Quarter. Rather unusual, because I lived most of my life in the suburbs of New Orleans, though my first apartment was on St. Ann Street smack dab in the middle of the Quarter. Anyway, I was sitting on the front porch of what was apparently my house with a bucket of scrub water and a broom. I was alone, and I remember I was sitting on the top step basking in the sun, thoroughly enjoying the heat and the sun's rays on my face. It was a different time period, sometime in the past; I assume it was in the 1800s. I was thinking about my herb gardens in the front yard that were planted between the azalea bushes and camellias, contemplating what else I was going to grow. I remember a strong fragrance of magnolia blooms, my absolute favorite flower of all times. It was a perfect dream that was about to get exponentially better.

In the distance I could hear the sound of hoofs clattering on the street made of bricks. Eventually, I could see over the bushes and through the trees that camouflaged part of the street a horse and buggy. There was a man at the helm, and he pulled right up to the front of my house. He climbed off of the wagon and reached into the back pulling

out a box, and started walking up the sidewalk towards me with box in hand. I recognized him. It was Doctor John, the infamous Gris Gris man, rootdoctor and healer.

In my dream, it felt as though I did not know him, but knew of him, as most people at that time did. He stood in front of me at the bottom of the steps and said in a deep voice "Good day. I believe this is for you." He held the box out to me and I walked down the steps and took it from him. I said "merci" and he winked and chuckled, turned and walked away. He got back in his wagon and drove off while I stood on the bottom step watching him.

I walked back up the steps and again sat on the top step and opened the box. Inside the box were a number of things and among those things was a bundle. I unwrapped the bundle and there was a small hurricane lamp, some herbs, roots and some other ingredients for making a magick lamp.

There were no written instructions but I knew what it was and what it was for. The creation of magick lamps in hoodoo is utilized by old-tyme rootworkers because they understand the power and effectiveness of magick lamps and how quickly they produce results. The reason they produce quick results is because they are hotter than candles and can be mounted by the Spirits. Once you recite a Saint's novena or utter the secret words of a Spirit over the lit lamp, you draw that Spirit down onto the work.

Here is the lamp given to me by Doctor John in my dream. Make this lamp when you are seeking healing, a business boost, protection, or help with drumming skills.

- Hurricane lamp
- Mineral oil

- Liquid camphor
- Lemon balm
- Sage
- Cloves
- Sassafras root
- Piece of leather
- Pipe tobacco
- High John root (the one in my dream was round)
- Bear root

For this lamp, you are going to write your petition on the piece of leather and attach it to the bottom of the wick with a safety pin. While lamps can be made using any number of receptacles, I use an actual hurricane lamp since that was the kind of vessel given to me in my dream. Focus on your intent and place a pinch of each herb and spice into the lamp, followed by the roots, pipe tobacco and liquid camphor. Fill the lamp 3/4 full with the mineral oil. Pull the wick about an inch clear from the receptacle and light. Adjust the flame to your liking and put the glass top onto the base. Ideally the lamp should be left to burn until your petition is realized. If you can't leave it lit, be sure to light it each day until your petition is realized. Top up the lamp with mineral oil each day. After nine days and after the work is done, you can take some of the oil in the lamp and use it as an anointing oil in rituals.

Note that many Hoodoo lamps involve the recitation of specific Psalms in their construction and activation; however, Doctor John was not a Christian (as far as I know) and so no Psalms were given. Feel free to use one if you wish; I don't think he would be offended.

This lamp can be tweaked to amplify a particular

purpose by choosing herbs and roots with the appropriate associations. Below are some suggestions for ingredients commonly used in Southern rootwork. You may use some or all of the ingredients listed and add to the above lamp. Note that after nine days, you can fill a small bottle with some of the oil and use as an anointing oil in rituals, to anoint altar items, instruments and Self.

Money

- Azalea flowers
- Five finger grass
- Parsley
- Alfalfa
- High John root
- Sassafras
- Ginger
- Cloves
- Cinnamon
- Brown sugar
- Maple syrup
- Molasses
- Cowry shells

Better Business

- Any of the money herbs and ingredients
- Lodestone
- Magnetic sand
- Silver dime
- 15 cents
- Dollar bill or other money

- Pyrite
- Brown sugar
- Almond oil
- Petition written on your business card

Protection

- Bear root
- Red brick dust
- Rue
- Hyssop
- Grave dirt from an ancestor or policeman
- Dirt from a police station or military base
- Evil eye bead
- Small mirror
- Snake sheds
- Ironwood
- Spanish moss
- Sage
- Cedar
- Alligator tooth
- Crab claw
- 23rd psalm written on parchment or torn out of a Bible

For drumming or other musical skill

- Crossroads dirt
- Chicken bone
- Guitar pick (for guitarists)
- Piece of written tablature folded three times towards you

- Snake sheds
- Piece of leather or goatskin
- Magnolia leaves and bark
- Lightning struck wood
- Red palm oil
- Dragon's blood resin
- Hard wood such as ironwood, oak, pine, cypress, maple or a piece of wood of the same type as your drum

Create this lamp with the lamp sitting on the Voudou vévé for drumming.

Healing

- Lavender
- Purple Coneflower
- Yarrow
- Bay laurel
- Roses
- Quartz crystal
- Lemon balm
- Pine resin
- Copal
- Myrrh
- Frankincense
- Petition written on parchment paper

To Sleep On The Tomb of Doctor John Montenet

© 2014 Witchdoctor Utu

While I live in the Niagara region of Ontario Canada, I serve the New Orleans Voodoo Spiritual Temple. After Hurricane Katrina made her devastating visit to the Crescent City, I was on one of the first flights into New Orleans after she was officially evacuated. I was there at the request of Priestess Miriam of the Temple, to help get it back up and running in time for Halloween, as well as essentially gut her house so restoration and rebuilding could begin. While the New Orleans Voodoo Spiritual Temple was spared harsh damage, her house was not so fortunate. Each day we worked at the house, and each night returned to the Temple where we slept and ate, only to start again the next day.

Monday, October 17th, 2005
The first day I arrived to help with the cleanup I did what I always do when landing in New Orleans, I went to St. Louis Cemetery Number 1 to pay my respects to the city's matron spirit and legendary Voodoo Queen Marie Laveau, as well the city's equally profound spirit of Doctor John Montenet.

I was shown the working tomb of Doctor John by members of the New Orleans Voodoo Spiritual Temple, and have worked at its location since 1999.

Since my first year visiting I was told of an old rite that was not easy to accomplish; to sleep upon Doctor John's tomb itself, all night long inside the cemetery. This would

bring about a much closer relationship with his spirit, enable blessings and conjures to be shared and received, a passage rite of devotion and gratitude, bravery and lunacy.

The neighborhood that surrounds St. Louis Cemetery Number 1 was extremely hostile for decades, at the best of times it was not wise to venture in or out of any other entrance than the one on Basin Street, most used by tour groups and tourists alike.

As I arrived on my trip to serve the Temple after Katrina's visit, I went to the cemetery. I was disappointed to see that the gate was locked. However now that the housing projects that surrounded the cemetery were abandoned post evacuation, I walked around the corner in relative safety and solitude to see the condition of the side gate, and much to my surprise and joy the gate was not even there, taken from the damage and water, the cemetery beckoned. As I walked through the cemetery that usually teems with tourists all day as well as workers, it was unlike any other time I walked its sacred grounds, I was alone in there, not another living soul. It was paradise and the silence allowed for thoughts and intentions not previously heard. I visited Marie Laveau to offer my condolences to her shrine and spoke to her of the work I was in the city to do.

Soon I was off to see the good doctor. I would say no more than two minutes at his door and shrine I heard the test, the challenge, for now there was relative safety in the area, there was an opened gate to the cemetery 24 hours a day, it was the perfect time to accept the challenge, to sleep for one night upon the working tomb of Doctor John Montenet. Consider the risks of this rite at any other time previous to Katrina; having to climb the wall of the cemetery to gain entrance, illegal and as stated earlier,

beyond dangerous, as many witnesses in the hostile hood would clearly see one go in, and many could quite possibly follow one in there for who knows what macabre reason. But the gate was not even attached to the wall, it was not even there, the projects abandoned, it was the time to do what I had wanted to achieve for many years. I would sleep on the Doctor's tomb.

SUNDAY, OCTOBER 30TH 2005; DEVIL'S NIGHT

After daily returning to the cemetery during breaks and early evening for visits and recon, it was Devil's Night that I would spend in St. Louis Number 1. While the projects were abandoned and evacuated, this was still not without danger. There was a curfew in order during those weeks, no one on the streets after 12 AM, no excuses and no reason would be accepted, if one was caught on the streets by the numerous army convoys patrolling the Quarter, one would be scooped up and taken away, the end, so once I was in there it was for keeps. There were of course still undesirables in the city too, lurking in the shadows for nefarious opportunities. It was evening; I walked past the New Orleans Police Department, now a home to the very officers banished from patrolling the Quarter because of corruption, thuggery and failure to secure safety for the residents that were there. It was in fact the New York State Troopers that patrolled the Quarter. I walked past their compound, barbecues cooking and rap music blaring. I waved as I walked by; it was only 8 PM or so, nothing to see here. As I walked in at dusk, I greeted the gate keeper, knocking at the entrance with my bag filled with rum, beer and tobacco to share and offer. I was in.

It started with time spent at Marie Laveau's tomb, the

guardian of the graves. I walked back and forth between her and Doctor John's tomb sharing offerings, prayers and intention. It eventually came to be bed time, not that much sleep would ensue. I made a bed of sorts upon the doctor's tomb, lay down and looked towards the sky. This was unlike any other sky in the city, probably the darkest it had been in several decades, other than the French Quarter there was no power in the city, darkness ruled. While seeing the stars that night, meteors shot across the sky, celestial anomalies that would not be possible to witness in other times danced. The heaviness eventually set in, spirit took over, and I was enveloped into his concrete tomb, becoming one with the cement and his intense presence...it seemed to last forever.

When dawn began to illuminate the day, the sun's warmth was celebrated, it was glorious. It was like a church service was to begin, myself the only human in the congregation. I finished off with placing the Doctor John card, from the *New Orleans Voodoo Tarot* deck, on the tomb along with fallen palm leaves and various flowery trinkets akin to a graveyard. His tomb was now a shrine, a testament to our time together that night, as well as every day previous. As I walked out of the cemetery, no less than 30 feet from me, lay an old black man who had also bedded down for the night between two tombs, this surprised me. He would have seen and heard everything I was doing in there, he must have thought many things watching a strange white man wander and commune with the spirits that night, and resting openly upon the tomb of the Doctor. I listened and accepted that he was a protector of sorts, a watcher and elder of the city who found solace in there, it was peaceful and safe, it was a blessing.

While I had felt the power of Doctor John for years, drummed for him and to him across the continent, it was that passage rite that made my connection to him one so profound and sacred it has never left my mind, and enters my thoughts often. I did it to honour Doctor John Montenet, to honour Priestess Miriam the New Orleans Voodoo Spiritual Temple, to honour Priest Oswan, I did it to honour Louis Martine; the Spiritual Doctor and Priest of the Temple, I did it to honour and connect with the drumming conjurers who came before me, those who had also endured the rite. That night with the blessings of Doctor John I entered an order, I received his conjures, I entered as a friend and left as family...he is a part of me, I entered his tomb.

(After Katrina, great areas of the city and parish were with electricity. Therefore, sleeping on Dr. John's tomb, Utu saw a sky similar to the the sky Dr. John looked to for messages, as indicated by Lafcadio Hearn, page 100. Starlight reigned upon New Orleans.)

Notes on the Painting of The Tomb of Doctor John

© 2014 Linda Falorio

Fred and I were in NO visiting Mishlen Linden and Louis Martinié for All Hallows Eve, 1993, when we chanced upon a wonderful black-headed djembe drum from Senegal while cruising the French Market. A quick visit to an ATM and purchase in hand, we joined Mishlen and Lu for a wonderful drumming event in Congo Square. A periodic event since around the late 18th Century celebrated by slaves

and free people of color alike, this day the drumming was led by master drummers, Luther and Kufaru.

The next day, *la Fête des Morts,* the day when families come together and go to the cemetery to honor their deceased relatives, we visited St. Louis No. 1 Cemetery to dedicate the Black Drum, led by Lu via funambulatory pathways known only to himself to the tomb of Doctor John Bokor. There the Black Drum was ritually presented with prayers, rites and supplications and graciously accepted by the good Doctor John.

Upon returning home, we found to our dismay that all carry-on luggage was required to prove that it would fit into a small rectangular box before being allowed aboard the plane – and there Fred was, carrying his djembe! No way would the 23" x 24" round-topped, goblet-shaped drum ever fit into that ridiculously small wire cage. As other passengers nervously queued, trusting to the protection of Doctor John, Fred effortlessly carried the now invisible Black Drum aboard the plane and rested it between his feet where it remained unnoticed for the flight home. The flight attendants seemed befuddled and confused when they saw us deplane with Fred carrying the Black Drum under his arm. The painting commemorates that significant event.

(The painting is reproduced on page 109. Also, its interesting to note that Lafcadio Hearn describes Dr. John as a native of Senegal, see page 95.)

Bringing Balance to the Order of Voodoo Religion

© 2014 Priestess Miriam
New Orleans Voodoo Spiritual Temple

This is in relation to the masculine role that Dr. John brought out, because to bring forth life we know life needs a masculine energy to intervene. So Dr. John balanced the wheel of the yin and the yang, we would call it the active to the passive. Here the active is the masculine and the passive is the feminine and so it took both those two energies to blend and to bring a concrete balance to the order of voodoo religion or mysticism. Bringing the mysteries together.

Priestess Miriam at her altar in
The New Orleans Voodoo Spiritual Temple

The Elevation of Dr. John Montane

© 2014 Andrieh Vitimus

Dr. John Montane is a critical and often untold part of the story of New Orleans Voodoo. At Starwood in 2012, I was part of a larger ritual created by Priest Louie Martinié to elevate Dr. John to the status of a Loa. This had been the second large ritual to elevate the spirit.

At the ritual, we had several members of my working group present. We were all dressed in white with red head wraps. I had brought my Papa Legba cane. Normally, at most public rituals or rituals at another Voodoo house, I tell all the students and members not to get possessed unless we are explicitly asked to engage in possessions. Priest Martinié invited me to assist in the ritual, which was a great honor.

The ritual was a New Orleans style ritual. The energy was crackling even at the start of the ritual. We went from the Bamboula into the calls to Legba and then something quite interesting happened. Louie explicitly motioned that he wanted us to get possessed. Legba possessed me and then one by one Legba possessed every member of my working group. The door was opening VERY wide indeed. In fact, Legba possessed others. In hindsight, I should have realized I may be witness to the partial birth of a new Loa in the tradition.

The ritual continued and the drumming continued increasing in power. We started dancing and drumming hard for Dr. John Montane. Louie had concentrated drums for that purpose (Dr. John was said to be a famous

drummer). Veves for Dr. John had been previously worked through. The energy was absolutely tangible, powerful and building. Something was coming. You could feel it in the air. It was there. The moment came.

I could feel Dr. John come to the threshold of the door that was open. It was like he, at this point, did not quite know how to interact or interface with multiple people at the same time. He was there however. As soon as I had those realizations, a couple of my students shook violently and fell down which is a sign of possession. One of my students fell down, shaking violently but rhythmically and was fully possessed. Doctor John had made it to the physical world fully. I ran over to the person to protect the person's head and body. I tested the possession and made sure the person did not get hurt. I could see that Louie was taking care of someone else in possession. The possession was absolutely real, you could feel the energy streaming off the person and it lasted more then a few minutes.

Often time, when you are first getting possessed by a new entity that is unknown to the horse, this seems to be the pattern. In my experience in Voodoo (and I am a priest), I have seen the possessions get more and more refined as the spirit and horse build a better and more complete interface. Falling down, shaking and having potentially little control over the body while in possession usually means the interface between the horse and the spirit has not been refined enough. In this case, I believe that part of the interface problem was on the spiritual side. Doctor John was also learning how to exist in multiple bodies at the same time, and how to step into a willing horse. I got the distinct impression that as more and more work possession rituals were attempted, that he would get better

at this part of the process. The mere fact, that he could cause verified possession by that point in time was a sure sign to me that he was ready to be elevated and ready to be born into this new and fantastic state.

From the ritual, I experienced there was no doubt in the power and efficacy of the ritual. It seemed like Doctor John had been born into the new state, but like a baby had to learn how to crawl and then walk. I am sure as the work with Dr. John continues; he will grow and become a most helpful, beneficial and extraordinary spirit to work with. Given the history of New Orleans Voodoo and his contribution to the current, this is truly a fitting and deserving honor for Dr. John to receive. Even participating, I personally learned a tremendous amount about the interface between spirit and the horse. I was doubly honored to see the progression of a most exceptional dead forefather move to a more exalted state. I hope in the near future, Dr. John has enough strength to travel and visit us in our temple. It was a tremendous experience, and I can not thank Louie enough for hosting it.

(Andrieh Vitimus can be reached via his website at andriehvitimus.com.)

SOME CONJURES

Louie Martinié

15, FEBRUARY, 1914: With Maegdlyn. .We both drank of the water kept on the altar for Dr. John. I drank and touched the back of my neck and forehead. Two Hi John Roots

consecrated with Elixir of Red Lion and White Eagle (Culling – GBG).

Expedition into Rorrim: The white snake springs from the abysmal waters and I startle. Again the white snake springs and I open. The snake has pierced my chest and I bleed through my heart. The blood flows through Blanc Dan-i to my children in the Invisible World. A white beam of light appears. My familiars and the powers that protect me drink deeply.

Dr. John indicates the small area directly under the front of his hat. Place a bit of water there.

Both roots placed in Dr. John's glass of water. Water turned a golden yellow.

23, FEBRUARY, '14:

Babalon with two hands. Annoint self with elixir. Strengthen Blanc Dan-i as conduit. A bridge of white light. This image of a bridge (Bridgette) opens a path to Manman Bridgette. Mishlen entered the temple during the working. Later she said that my cotton shirt was too hot for her to touch.

4, MARCH, '14, MARDI GRAS

At the invitation of Jessica Radcliff, walked with Society of Saint Cecilia, the patron saint of music, to the Mississippi to make offerings and to honor what has passed into the arms of the ancestors in the past year.

Offerings: A conjure composed of absinthe, water and earth from St. Roch Cemetery, a bit of bread from a meal with the present Dr. John (Mac). Dr. John Montanee's signature. A black rock from Manman Bridgette's altar. A white bead (snake egg).

A wonder full parade wove its way through the wet and cold to the river. I made my offerings and the signature of Dr. John unfurled upon hitting the water and floated with his name upright as if looking back at us. Dr. John is revived by the water. I passed the selves that I wore this past year into the ancestor's arms.

Expedition into Rorrim: Dr. John floats just beneath the Waters. Black coat and white shirt drift slightly in the rivers flow. He reaches up and takes his signature. Presses it to his chest and opens his mouth. A thousand bubbles move from his lips to the surface and are received by the air. Each bubble a blessing bursting sweetly upon those who march in second line with Saint Cecilia.

On going remembrance of Dr. John and his retinue I do daily:

"To you Dr. John". .I take a drink. .tap signature rhythm of Bamboula.

"To you John Montanee". .I take a drink. .tap signature rhythm of Bamboula

"To you Joey and those drummers who have come after". .I take a drink. .tap signature rhythm of Bamboula.

I like this in that it distinguishes between Dr. John and John Montanee. Dr. John is a title, a creation of John Montanee. A projection thrown by time and remembering into the rarified aires where loa are born. John Montanee is the foundation supporting a sure path to Dr. John. He is the man who dared to eat peaches.

Joey is a Temple Drummer who passed into the arms of the ancestors.

(A video demonstrating the Bamboula rhythm is available for

viewing on BlackMoonPublishing.com/videos and the drum notation which appears in A Priest's Head, A Drummer's Hands, *pages 36 & 37, is available as well.)*

A Dream and a Ritual Record

© 2014 Maegdlyn

I once had a dream that was so vivid that to this day I am somewhat convinced that it is true. In my dream Louis and I are doing research at the public library of New Orleans. We come across a document that has a record of a marriage between John Montanee, and his wife at a particular church. We look it up on a map and it is still in existence on a particular street in New Orleans. We drive to the church, and it is a tall regal looking building, made of grey stone, with huge stained glass windows. As we walk up to it, we realize that the windows are all boarded up. We try to peek through the glass but it is extremely dusty on the inside and there is no way to gain access.

BABALON RISING 2012: Night ritual to Dr. John in which Phil Farber activates the aspect of ATEM, a heightened level of awareness, designed to encourage communion with spirits. During the ritual, my eyes became heavy and I felt as if my body became older and had aching joints. I became fascinated with the star patterns, and realized that they felt different than the ones that I (he) had seen in his youth. I got the sense that he was very familiar with the constellations and their location in the sky, and that these constellations represented a new world, a different

perspective. This was also accompanied by a sense of acceptance and peace but tinged with sadness and loss.

I'm not sure where this last perception comes from as it has grown within my head until it is a conglomeration of impressions. There is a small house with two front parlor rooms and several bedrooms in the back. There is a second building in the back yard, with chickens and livestock in the yard in between. There are children running around in the back, and a kitchen that faces into the back yard. In the front, it seems to be a form of brothel, yet it is clean and has a positive energy. There are several women, I do not know how many, they are very young, and Dr. John swings one of them around in his arms. She is lighter skinned than he is and she is laughing. There is a man sitting on the porch in the shade, and he is drunk but in a good mood. He is playing some sort of music but I can't tell what it is...

You Can Be a Healer Now

© 2014 Baron Sylvia

Dr. John Ritual, Babalon Rising 2012

The altar was set up with drums and offerings. I brought my doll who looks like the happiest little drummer boy to the altar for Baby Ghede.
    The ritual started. Those with rattles, myself included, started an inner circle around the altar. The drummers gathered in an outer circle. This was not planned, but I found this lineup to be perfect.

The ritual progressed and I saw dancers go into trances. I guarded one that was not yet mounted by Dr. John. I watched as the one who was mounted enjoy water offerings. It wasn't long before the dancer I was watching over became mounted by Dr. John.

I could see his calm face and eyes through her face and eyes. He stretched out his/her feet to me. He spoke to me.; "My feet are so sore, take your asson and sooth them." I sat and gently shook my rattle over the very visible swollen feet and ankles of the mounted dancer.

I watched him close his eyes and smile as the swelling went down. He spoke before departing; " You see now you know how to heal, you can be a healer now."

I felt incredibly blessed he would grant me such ability as to be able to heal others.

He Walked From His House

© 2014 Houngan Steven Denney

We talked about Dr. Jon's house. He often walked from his house due south along the road, then turned right, walking west, down the rampart. Sometimes he would cut thru the trees and brush, walking due west from his house, carrying bags of certain jars...there are several children walking with him, carrying sacks of glass bottles, branches and leaves.

A Dream

© 2014 Pamela Marie Nemec

I dreamt of Dr. John and celebrating. There was a great crowd walking through the cemetery with living persons and Spirits amongst them. The air was a bit stagnant due to its warmth but then a swirl of wind began. The Spirits swayed back and forth as a float appeared in a Mardi Gras form. There were little flags edging the float adorned in sparkly metallic ribbons. They represented the colors of Mardi Gras in purples, greens, and deep yellows.

The float emanated diverse cultures and magic. It floated through the cemetery then out into the streets where the people and Spirits began to get energy from the earth. I saw Louie Martinié dancing amidst the crowd in the streets but he seemed alone personally and in his thoughts. I turned and asked Priestess Miriam what this was about, she just nodded but I knew it was the celebration of the dead.

— Dec 30, 2010

Drum Needed to be Played

© 2014 Midnyte Hierax

Babalon Rising; Ritual

I got the impression that he was very pleased to see those who were tranced out - it was an almost positively gleeful feeling. I also remember the impression that the large drum (sitting on its side with the statue on it) HAD to be played.

During the Mami Wata call, I think I actually heard that drum playing by itself, and then later it just needed to be played. I also found myself wanting to go around and touch/play other drums.

Sweet, Sweet Water
2012 Babalon Rising Festival: Conjure

© 2014 Sara Grey

The drums. Those voices of the Loa. They called me, broke my heart, scattered it and rebuilt it there on the spot. I knew that I had to answer. No was not an option. Is it ever an option when you are called? I don't think so. History is full of stories of people resisting the call and ending in misfortune. I would go. I had to, my feet led the way. I had to go to where the drums beat and the waters speak. This is the call to service.

I was dancing, spinning, listening to the drums, lost in the sounds and I spun right out of myself. I remember looking someone in the eyes, she was going to put some water (?) on all of us. I spun around her and it was this spin I lost myself in. I was in the backseat driver of my body. It was the most beautiful and terrifying sensation. Things get a little hazy at this point.

At some point I/He drop to our knees in front of a sacred drum altar. It is then He settles in the driver's seat a little better. We are operating as one. A horse and rider. We get up and reverse direction. We rode the current of the drums, the energy of the dancers. It was important to move the opposite direction to simulate the vibrations of

the music that the dancers moved on. We did a few circles then dropped again.

We called for water. Sweet, sweet water.

I lose time and I know I am safe and that this is an honor. I feel the thirst, the unending need for water. I am on my knees, hands in the air, hands on the earth, hearing maracas in my ears. The sound is grating to the spirit. He wants to throw the maracas. He likes the drums. My/his hands and arms are twined in the earth, up in the air, and wrapped around a bottle of water. He drank the sacred cemetery water, He drank bottled water. An urgent need for water. This thirst, like fire, it caught in my throat, the throat ached, my eyesight was poor. He just wanted water, his thirst needed to be quenched and it was unending.

At some point the ritual ends. Florida water is applied to me and words are said to try and coax me back into the front seat. I settle firmly. I am tired, and covered in water. People ask if I am alright, and I nod Yes. I am more then alright. I am euphoric and I feel like I exist out of time. I laugh a little and my husband helps me stumble off into the night to rest.

(At the time of the conjure, Sara Grey did not know Bright's disease was associated with intense thirst.)

Voices of the Community
Investigations

Bright's Disease
A Medical Investigation

© Copyright 2014 Sara Grey

(Please see John Montanee's Certificate of Death, pages 62-63.)

The disease was discovered in 1872 by Richard Bright when he noticed that patient's with Dropsy (Edema, Swelling) had kidney damage when he performed the autopsy. When the disease was diagnosed it was considered incurable and fatal. Usually by the time the disease was detected it was in the advanced stages. Emily Dickinson, the famous poet, also died of this disease. In my research, I am also running into other deceased occultists that have died from Bright's.

The disease was treated with blood lettings that were induced by 'cuppings' applied to the chest and lower back (where kidney pain can often be felt). A diuretic or laxative could possibly have been used. It was treated with Calomel and with remedies that contained Camphor, Magnesium Sulfate, and Potassium Supertartrate. Sometimes Ipecac was used (it induces vomiting). Diet would have been restricted to balance the blood and taking the waters (warm baths) could have been recommended. Some patients were advised to wear only flannel and these treatments were continued until the early 20th century when diagnostic techniques became better. The name of the disease only changed then,

when the diagnostics became better.

Presently, Bright's disease is a vague and obsolete term for kidney disease. It usually refers to inflammatory or degenerative kidney disease, marked by blood in the urine, protein in the urine, and sometimes edema (swelling), hypertension (high blood pressure), fatigue, and nitrogen retention. Symptoms include cough or shortness of breath, diarrhea, excessive urination, fever, loss of appetite, joint or muscle aches, and nosebleeds. It is commonly called Nephritis (Kidney Inflammation) and it moves into Kidney failure.

At that point in his life, Dr. John would have had the symptoms of kidney failure (end stage renal disease) and hypertension. The symptoms of chronic kidney failure are appetite loss, general ill feeling and fatigue, headaches, itching (pruritus) and dry skin, nausea, weight loss without trying to lose weight. When kidney function gets worse, other symptoms may develop. These include abnormally dark or light skin, bone pain, brain and nervous system symptoms: drowsiness and confusion, problems concentrating or thinking, numbness in the hands, feet, or other areas, muscle twitching or cramps, breath odor, easy bruising, bleeding or blood in the stool, excessive thirst, frequent hiccups, low level of sexual interest and impotence, shortness of breath, sleep problems, such as insomnia, restless leg syndrome, and obstructive sleep apnea, swelling of the feet and hands (edema), and vomiting, typically in the morning.

Symptoms of Hypertension are severe headache, fatigue or confusion, vision problems, chest pain, difficulty breathing, irregular heartbeat, blood in the urine, pounding in the chest, neck, or ears.

During the ritual on the June 8th, 2012, I experienced extreme thirst and in the ritual on the 7th, the night before, I experienced difficulty breathing.

References

Empowher. (n.d.). End Stage Renal disease (ESRD) Information, Symptoms and Treatments on Yahoo! Health. Retrieved June 11, 2012, from http://health.yahoo.net/channel/end-stage-renal-disease-esrd.html (no longer available)

Glomerulonephritis: MedlinePlus Medical Encyclopedia. (n.d.). National Library of Medicine - National Institutes of Health. Retrieved June 11, 2012, from http://www.nlm.nih.gov/medlineplus/ency/article/000484.htm

Glomerulonephritis: Symptoms - MayoClinic.com. (n.d.). Mayo Clinic. Retrieved June 11, 2012, from http://www.mayoclinic.com/health/glomerulonephritis/DS00503/DSECTION=symptoms

High Blood Pressure Symptoms - Hypertension Symptoms. (n.d.). Web MD. Retrieved June 11, 2012, from www.webmd.com/hypertension-high-blood-pressure/guide/hypertension-symptoms-high-blood-pressure

Kidney failure, chronic: Symptoms-MayoClinic.com. (n.d.). Mayo Clinic. Retrieved June 11, 2012, from http://www.mayoclinic.com/health/kidney-failure/DS00682/DSECTION=symptoms

Prevention. (n.d.). Chronic Renal Failure (CRF) Information, Symptoms and Treatments on Yahoo! Health. Retrieved June 11, 2012, from http://health.yahoo.net/channel/chronic-renal-failure-crf.html (no longer available)

Venes, D., & Taber, C. W. (2009). Taber's cyclopedic medical dictionary (21st ed.). Philadelphia: F.A. Davis Co.

The Superposition of Dr. Jean
A Handwriting Investigation

© 2014 Denise Alvarado

My experiences with Dr. Jean began many years ago when I was still a teenager. But, it wasn't until recently that I realized who this person was who made himself available to me for advice and guidance during a time in my life when I needed it very much.

He was someone I would see walking the park; he was an elderly man, gray hair, and usually alone; although, sometimes I would see him sitting on a park bench or standing beneath a tree speaking to someone one on one. There was something about him that drew me to him. I think part of it was that I thought he was homeless; yet, he always seemed okay, despite living on some of the harshest streets in America. I left him offerings of food on a number of occasions; I knew where he spent time, and behind a bank was one such place. So, during holidays I would make him up a plate and leave it there for him.

Once, I mustered up enough courage to approach him. It was 1977 at the time and I had just gotten back from

Europe where I had experienced a life changing event. I felt lost and alone. I had met someone who would turn out to be the worst relationship of my life and who was trying to impose an extreme view of what it meant to live life as a Christian. When I approached him, I introduced myself. He smiled and I asked him if we could talk. He nodded affirmatively, and we talked for a while. I shared with him what was going on in my life and told him I was looking to make sense of it all. He said life is full of mysteries, and it is our life experiences that unlock the mysteries for us. I remember him speaking about faith, and walking through life in faith that the unseen spirits would take care of me. Other than that I don't remember the content of our conversation, it was so long ago. But I can say that he was as real as anyone else I have spoken to on this physical plane.

When we were done talking, I thanked him and turned to walk away. Then, I remembered I hadn't even asked him his name, so I stopped and turned around and said, "I'm sorry, I never even asked you your name." He said, "They call me John."

I walked back to my car, got in and began driving away in the opposite direction from where we were. About two blocks in the opposite direction from where I had left John standing, there he was, walking towards me. I thought to myself, that's John! But I just left him back there, how could he be two blocks away when he was back there? But that was him and there he was, obviously in two places at the same time. It blew my mind. It was at that moment I knew I had not been talking to a man but with the spirit of a man, a very special man, and his name was John.

Was this John the Doctor Jean Montenee?

According to quantum physics, microscopic systems can be in two or more places at the same time, a principle called superposition aka quantum weirdness. And while it has been discovered since 1977 that atoms and electrons can be in two places at one time, and even molecules in plants and cells in birds share this characteristic, it has yet to be discovered as a trait in human beings. But this wasn't quantum physics – or was it? Whatever it was, I never forgot the experience.

Many, many years later I was again going through something very traumatic that was playing out in the public arena. Without going into details, he made himself known to my perpetrator in a way that I would certainly recognize it was him. And, he was showing up to me in a variety of ways: I had published an article about him by Alyne Pustanio, someone had special-ordered an altar doll of him, Louie Martinié had told me he had located his grave site, and someone had sent me an obscure video about the Widow Paris in which he played a prominent character in the storyline. In short, a multitude of coincidental things happened during a short span of time where Doctor Jean's presence was amplified.

All of these things made me reflect back to my experience those many moons ago in New Orleans when I met that mystical John who could be in more than one place at one time, the one who told me to have faith that the spirits would take care of me and that my life experiences would unlock the mysteries for me. It was at this time that I put two and two together; that John then was the same Jean that lived in the 1800s and the same Jean that is being elevated today, in New Orleans, in this book, by the drummers and the singers and the holders of the mysteries of New

Orleans Voudou. I understand now that what is seemingly impossible is very possible, and when we welcome Doctor Jean Montenee, he will come.

Getting to Know Him

Not much is known about Doctor Jean, and I want to know more about him. Other than the infamous obituary written by Lafcadio Hearn called "Last of the Voudous," there is very little else, with the exception of the work by Louie Martinié. In the book A Priest's Head, a Drummer's Hands, there is a prayer to Dr. Jean and an image of a document with his signature on it. I got the idea to try a rather unorthodox method of discovering more information about him. I decided to analyze his handwriting.

Handwriting analysis is a powerful tool for learning about yourself and other people. With a mere signature, we can see what makes a person tick, determine their personality characteristics, and evaluate what potential obstacles stand in their way. Handwriting analysis is routinely used as a compatibility tool for relationships and as a forensic tool for developing criminal profiles and cracking forgery cases. When done correctly, it can be a fabulous supplemental tool for enhancing psychic readings and divinations as well.

Most graphologists reject the application of handwriting analysis to the supernatural and the occult. What I am suggesting here is not the false presentation of graphology as some sort of mystical, psychic gift or method of fortune-telling. I am suggesting that it can be used as a practical tool for enhancing and confirming or disconfirming information received through more traditional methods. If it works for living people, why can't it work for someone

who has passed?

There are some basic ways to interpret styles, slants, loops, sizes and spaces in signatures and handwriting samples that reveal truths about personality and character. This is because humans project themselves in everything they do. Handwriting is just an extension of the brain and if you know what to look for, you can get a pretty good idea about how a person ticks from observing how they sign their name. According to handwriting analyst Gary Thomas, in addition to creating a complete personality profile from a handwriting sample, you can learn a slew of other things about a person, such as their health issues, morality, past experiences, hidden talents, and mental problems. This type of information lends itself perfectly to spiritual work. I became more and more excited the more I thought about trying this method to confirm what is known and not known about Doctor Jean. Doctor Jean Montanee (Montanet) aka Doctor John, Bayou John, and a slew of versions on a name theme, is the original gris gris man of New Orleans. He is said to have mentored Marie Laveaux in the art of gris gris. He is known to have been quite wealthy at one point with a thriving business as a rootdoctor specializing in herbal remedies and gris gris. Unfortunately, he was not well-schooled in the ways of business legalities, and he was eventually tricked into creating and signing documents that literally gave away all of his property, leaving him penniless.

In a rare document that appeared in Louis Martinié's *A Priest's Head, A Drummer's Hands, New Orleans Voodoo: An Order of Service* (2010) (also appearing in this grimoire on pages 44 and 46), we have a great sample of his signature at the very bottom. We can analyze the sample and gain

a glimpse into aspects of his character that perhaps have yet to be revealed, or may simply reinforce what is already thought to be true about him.

In reality, little is known about Doctor Jean. He is said to have been charismatic, intelligent and driven with an entrepreneurial spirit. Does his handwriting confirm these observations?

PRESSURE: While it's difficult to tell for sure from the sample, it appears Doctor John wrote with average to heavy pressure. The amount of pressure applied when a person writes is an indicator of emotional energy. Writers with heavy pressure are usually highly successful. This handwriting sample from Doctor John reveals a person with a high energy level and a propensity for success. This seems to be consistent with what we know about his life.

BASELINE: A normal baseline is slightly wavy, almost straight but not perfectly so. This indicates someone with an even temperament who is emotionally stable and grounded. In someone who survived slavery, this characteristic would be evidence of resiliency.

SLANT: A right slant indicates a person who is emotional, caring, warm and outgoing and their lives are governed by their hearts as opposed to their heads. From the little that has been written about Doctor John, we know he was quite gregarious, possessed a magnetic personality and had a big heart. It is said that Doctor John regularly distributed gumbo and jambalaya to the poor, and continued this act of kindness throughout his life – during the height of his success, as well as during his lowest of lows.

By some accounts, he was not a very trusting person, particularly of Whites (not surprising). As the story goes, however, he asked a friend of his to teach him how to read and write with the thought that he would be able to conduct business with confidence. Some say that once he learned how to sign his name, he was signing everything put in front of him without understanding what it actually meant to sign something. This type of behavior could be driven by trust in those who he was reportedly doing business with. Perhaps it was simple ignorance. Or, it could be fueled by a sense of grandiosity – "showing off," as it were. Whatever the reason, when it was noticed that he was signing all kinds of things and making all kinds of deals, some unscrupulous individuals took advantage of him and used this behavior in the orchestration of his downfall. Signing away most of his fortune coupled with a reported fondness for gambling eventually left him penniless, or so it is said.

SIZE: The oversized first letter of his signature, presumably a "J", shows Doctor Jean took great pride in his family. It also indicates a sense of importance or "larger than life" life. We know that Doctor Jean reportedly had 15 wives, married according to traditional African ritual by some reports; others say he procured his wives by purchasing them as slaves. As he was a freeman, he was able to own slaves legally.

SHAPE: The shape of Doctor Jean's signature is quite interesting and rather flamboyant. The first letter is not only large, it is also circular. Large first letters show a strong desire to appear in public and a need to be in control.

Large letters written in an original style also signify an innovative personality and someone who possesses strong leadership abilities.

Legibility: Dr. Jean's signature is not very legible. This may be because he wasn't someone who wrote his whole life and only learned to sign his name as an adult. From the sample, my educated guess is that he signed his name Jean – likely using the French spelling of John given he was in New Orleans at a time when French was the dominant language. But, the image is not clearly legible by any stretch of the imagination. When someone signs an important document illegibly, it could be construed that they do not consider the signature to be of much importance and signing their name is purely a formality with little meaning. The actual spoken agreement is important, not the signature on a piece of paper. I cannot say with certainty that this is the case with Dr. Jean, but I rather suspect it is not far from the truth.

Placement of the signature: Signing a document in the middle, as opposed to on the left or right side, indicates someone who wants to be noticed as important. Dr. Jean signed his name pretty close to the middle of the document, and given other revelations about his self-image and sense of self-importance, it is consistent with the profile developed.

Summary of Dr. Jean's Personality Profile

Before I draw my picture of Dr. Jean, it is only fair to disclose that I am highly trained in psychological projective

testing and diagnostics, and this background no doubt informs my suggested profile. Still, it is the information I observed from his signature that forms the basis of the profile.

After examining Dr. Jean's signature, I suggest that he was a driven and industrious man, who had a desire to not only do well and adjust to the events of his life - as someone who was stolen, sold as a slave and forcibly moved to a different country (Cuba) as a result – but, to do exceedingly well. He no doubt suffered from terrible trauma, and his way of dealing with it was to master whatever task it was he was told to do. It is said he was either a Bambaran prince or the son of a Bambaran prince, and if this is the case, the effect on him, his ego, and his sense of importance would have been devastating on a different level than someone who was not a leader with a huge responsibility to his community. I am not suggesting that his trauma would be more than another African stolen from their family and homeland, just different with an additional layer.

Sometimes when a person becomes legendary they cease to be human beings and instead become the legend themselves. Dr. Jean is remembered according to his legend, as a powerful gris gris man who was rich, got a lot of women and who was the teacher of Marie Laveaux. The whole context of the trauma of the Diaspora is left completely out of his-story, and this is not only unfortunate, but it is highly disrespectful. My belief is that his goal from the onset of becoming a slave would have been to reclaim his personal power and power within the community (whatever community he ended up in), and to do so using his strength and charisma. This internal fortitude was enough to achieve

his eventual freedom from slavery; it is said that his West Indian master taught him to be an excellent cook and grew quite fond of him, and eventually gave him the gift of freedom. As a result, Dr. Jean left Cuba to be a cook on a ship and eventually ended up in New Orleans where these characteristics of strength, charisma and fortitude landed him as a gang leader of cotton rollers. Within that community, he began to be known for his apparent supernatural powers and fortune telling abilities. This set the tone for his eventual great success in New Orleans. All through the various narratives of his-story, we can see his ability to transcend the normal performance of a given task and exceed all expectations.

Dr. Jean was likely a man who liked to make grand entrances in an effort to make his presence known. But, he more than likely retreated from this showy demeanor to a very warm and gregarious human being. People probably liked him more than not and he likely had many friends, and at least as many acquaintances. He would have been someone who would have started a family as soon as possible and given the culture from which he came, would likely have had more than one wife and many children. Family would have been very important to him and he would have taken his role as provider very seriously – yet another mechanism to drive his entrepreneurial spirit.

In addition to being successful in his various jobs and as a provider, he would have taken his role as a leader of the Voudous quite seriously, as well. As gris gris is a religiomagical system originating in Senegal and practiced by the priests, it makes perfect sense that he would have brought knowledge of the tradition with him to New Orleans. Gris gris is one of the most unique characteristics

of New Orleans Voudou and a tradition that persists to this day - his contribution to the New Orleans religion is unsurpassed. He expected to be noticed and he was, as his legacy lives on in the heart of the Mysteries and can be heard and felt in the beat of every drum.

Beyond his need for recognition and the importance of his role in the development of New Orleans Voudou as we know it today, he would have also been a great healer. He was connected to others on a personal level and would have had a genuine concern for their wellbeing. He would have helped people who asked, and would have also figured out how to make money doing the very thing that created an air of mystique around him. Thanks to Dr. Jean and Marie Laveaux, New Orleans Voudou and Hoodoo continues to afford many people the opportunity to make a living today, as it did in the past.

Not much was ever written about Dr. Jean from firsthand accounts, at least that I am aware of. The most well-known piece of written literature was his obituary written by Lafcadio Hearn in 1885. Here is an excerpt of his obituary from *An American Miscellany*, vol. II, (1924) originally published in Harper's weekly, November 7th, 1885:

> *In the death of Jean Montanet, at the age of nearly a hundred years, New Orleans lost, at the end of August, the most extraordinary African character that ever gained celebrity within her limits. Jean Montanet, or Jean La Ficelle, or Jean Latanié, or Jean Racine, or Jean Grisgris, or Jean Macaque, or Jean Bayou, or "Voudoo John," or "Bayou John," or "Doctor John" might well have been termed "The Last of the Voudoos"; not that the strange association with which he*

was affiliated has ceased to exist with his death, but that he was the last really important figure of a long line of wizards or witches whose African titles were recognized, and who exercised an influence over the colored population. Swarthy occultists will doubtless continue to elect their "queens" and high-priests through years to come, but the influence of the public school is gradually dissipating all faith in witchcraft, and no black hierophant now remains capable of manifesting such mystic knowledge or of inspiring such respect as Voudoo John exhibited and compelled. There will never be another "Rose," another "Marie," much less another Jean Bayou.

It may reasonably be doubted whether any other Negro of African birth who lived in the South had a more extraordinary career than that of Jean Montanet. He was a native of Senegal, and claimed to have been a prince's son, in proof of which he was wont to call attention to a number of parallel scars on his cheek, extending in curves from the edge of either temple to the corner of the lips. This fact seems to me partly confirmatory of his statement, as Berenger-Feraud dwells at some length on the fact that the Bambaras, who are probably the finest Negro race in Senegal, all wear such disfigurations. The scars are made by gashing the cheeks during infancy, and are considered a sign of race. Three parallel scars mark the freemen of the tribe; four distinguish their captives or slaves. Now Jean's face had, I am told, three scars, which would prove him a free-born Bambara, or at least a member of some free tribe allied to the Bambaras, and living upon their territory. At all events, Jean possessed physical characteristics answering to those by which the French ethnologists in Senegal distinguish the Bambaras. He was of middle height, very strongly built, with broad shoulders, well-developed muscles, an inky black skin, retreating forehead, small bright eyes, a very flat nose,

and a woolly beard, gray only during the last few years of his long life. He had a resonant voice and a very authoritative manner...

The picture Hearn paints of Dr. Jean is consistent with the characteristics exhibited in his signature. While certain aspects are more than likely exaggerated in true Lafcadio Hearn style, the underlying truth is there. Dr. Jean was a strong, successful and highly influential man who has since risen to the status of loa in the very religion he helped to create. Dr. Jean Montanee is the Father of New Orleans Voodoo.

References

Gardner, R. (2002). *Instant Handwriting Analysis: A Key to Personal Success* (1st ed.), Llewellyn Publications.

Martinié, L. (2010). *A Priest's Head, A Drummer's Hands: New Orleans Voodoo; Order of Service.* Black Moon Publishing.

Dr. John Montanee:
An Astrological Riddle

© 2014 Rev. Bill Duvendack

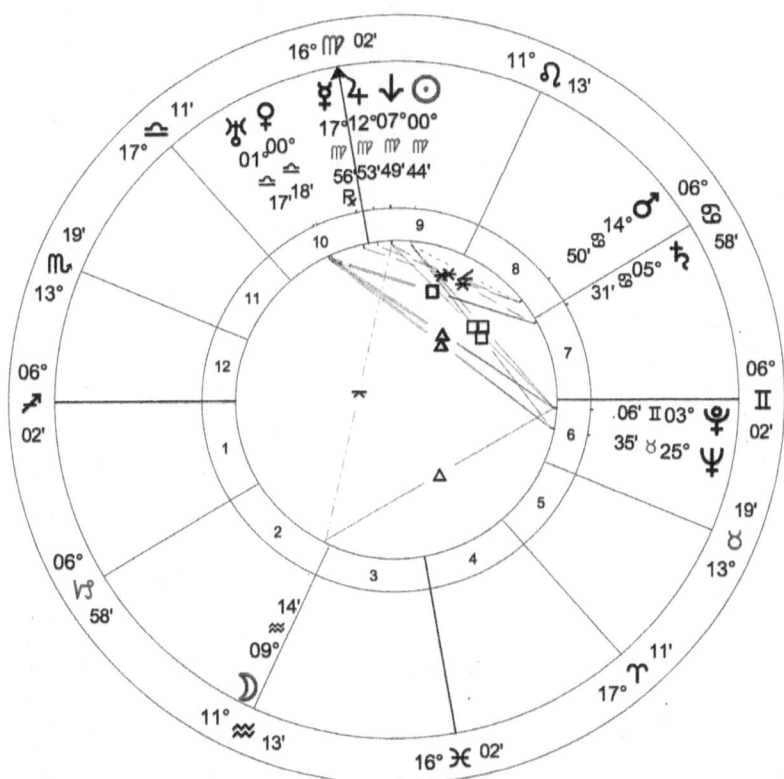

Dr. John Montanee's Astrological Death Chart
Male Chart, Aug. 23, 1885, NS Sun, 1:00 pm CST +6:00
New Orleans, Louisiana, 29° N57' 16" 090° W041' 30"
Geocentric, Tropical, Placidus, Mean Node, Rating:AA

While the above chart looks at where things were at the time of Dr. John's transition into spirit, I would like to take a few moments to explain why this chart was

used, instead of a birth chart, which is more traditional. Dr. John was born in Senegal, and arrived in North America afterwards, as a free man. As is commonly the case throughout history, there are no records of his birth that I am aware of, and this is a logical situation that I have seen more times than not, not only due to the era during which this occurred, but also due to the place where he was born. I state this here as an observation only, but it does leave us in a bind when it comes to figuring out what his birth chart might look like. The fact that there is conflicting information regarding his death complicates matters quite a bit, so in these following words I will share my logic and rationale, as well as insights into what his astrological chart may look like.

In astrology, there is a technique known as chart rectification that is basically a system to deduce the birth time of an individual when a time is not known, or suspected to be incorrect. However, to my knowledge, this process doesn't extend very easily to figuring out a birth date. For an astrological chart, the prerequisite information is the individual's birth month, day, year, place, and time. In the case of Dr. John, all we have is a birth place; no time, no day, and no year. This lack of information is further complicated by the fact that his death certificate for 1885 has him listed as "Aged 70 years," yet his obituary states that he was close to 100 years old. (*The Last of the Voudoos*, Lafcadio Hearn, page 94. This article is widely acknowledged as Dr. John's functional obituary.) As can be seen, the idea of being close to 100 years old can be widely interpreted. Does this mean that the obituary writer knows something that the person filling out the death certificate didn't know, or does this mean that the individual that

wrote the obituary treats being 70 years old as "close to 100 years old?" With the average life span of an individual being shorter during that time, it would be easy to see how 70 years of age could be considered close to 100 years old. Hence, immediately, we have conflict between the obituary and the death chart. This further complicates matters regarding the year he was born, and makes things very difficult indeed.

The second concept that complicates things is the fact that the death certificate simply states that he was 70 years of age. The tricky part of this is that we don't know if he had turned 70 years old earlier in the year or he still had a birthday later in the year. This means that if you use the death certificate as the beginning point, he could either be born in late 1814 or sometime in 1815, before August 23rd, which is the date of his death. However, even though this complication is present, it can still provide a lot of insight that we can work with, so let's begin our analysis. I'll do my best to break everything down into easy to understand language because sometimes astrology can be a foreign language, and it is not my intent to confuse the reader with such unique terms that are in astrology. If anyone is interested in the more technical side of astrology regarding him, please contact me, for this is a fascinating case study for me.

The data that we have at our disposal to work with is the following: 1) Death Certificate, 2) Marriage Certificate, 3) the knowledge that he had Bright's disease, 4) the knowledge that he was born in Senegal, Africa, 5) the knowledge that he had many lovers and children. From an astrological perspective, this really isn't much material to work with, but I have been able to deduce some usable

information. We've already discussed the issues with the death certificate when put into context with the obituary, so I won't go into it further here, so let's move on to point #2: his marriage certificate. In astrology, significant events like marriages can be forecasted and/or worked with to discover more information about an individual. Usually, marriages occur when there is a particular transit that is occurring in the chart of the native. The second factor to take into account is *progressions*. A transit is when a body in the sky (planet, Sun, etc.) is moving through a certain area of an astrological chart, known as a house. A house in an astrological chart is simply a life area, so in this case, the life area of Dr. John has to do with intimate relationships and marriages. Without going into too much detail, a progression is where a chart body has moved to, from its natal placement. Yes, the chart grows and changes as we grow and change, yet the original birth chart remains the same, so the situation becomes layered. Hence when looking at events like marriages, we look to see what planet (this includes the Sun and the Moon) was moving through his house of marriage and intimate relationships (the 7th house of an astrological chart), and we *progress* his chart to that day for more information. I'll make this clearer soon, but simply for now it is enough to note because I want to impress upon you how this information is valuable and applicable to the situation.

His condition of Bright's disease was of immense value when researching his birth time. Here again, without going into too many astrological technicalities, let me just say that there are correspondences in medical astrology that tell us what to look for as indicators of such a disease. In other words, this disease gives a further clue as to what

astrological factors were present in his birth chart. The fact that he was born in Senegal, Africa is self explanatory when put into context of what has been discussed, but even though we know it was Senegal, we don't know the specific area or town, so it is only of partial use. Quite frankly I chose Simenti out of convenience, but the actual area he was from matters quite a bit, and can affect things like the astrological houses significantly.

What this information reveals are key factors to look for to deduce his birthday. When I began playing around with different dates that meet the astrological criteria, I did arrive at some possibilities for birth dates. I will be the first to say that these are "ball park" estimates, but given the information I have available, and my astrological skill, I feel confident that they are as accurate as they can be, without further information available. The dates that we deduce are the following: October 29th & 30th, 1814, or April 11, 1815. Both of these are strong possibilities, and if they're off by a few days, then so be it.

If his death certificate is to be trusted as being accurate when it says that he was aged 70 years, then the above dates can be strongly considered. In astrology, the planets Sun through Saturn are known as the personal planets because they correspond to us on a day to day basis, so to speak, and our life cycles. While this is an excellent tool to work with in our day to day lives, this doesn't do us much good in this case because they move too fast to be of much use. However, the trans-Saturnian planets do reveal much insight as to who he was from an astrological perspective. Let's take a closer look at his astrological character traits, then, and see what they reveal!

To begin with, he would have had a lot of emphasis on long

distance travel and all concepts related to being influenced by foreign lands, foreign cultures, foreign belief systems, and foreign people. This is corroborated by the fact that he was taken from Senegal to New Orleans, and his spirituality was a blend of those two influences. In astrologese, this is evidenced by his Uranus and Neptune being in Sagittarius. Sagittarius is also the sign of spirituality, which played a major role in his life. Also of note is the influence of Pisces in his chart, reflected by Pluto and Chiron. Pisces is a water sign, which means that he would have been a strongly emotional person, which is further corroborated by his many loves, grandiose entrances, and children. However, Pisces is also the sign of the psychic, and the visionary, which were also key marks of his life. Jupiter, the planet of great beneficence, was in the sign of Libra, which is the sign of harmonious relationships and enjoying all of the beautiful things in life. Living large and appearing larger than life are two key phrases that come to mind here; both of which he is said to have exhibited during his lifetime. This is where the common traits between the two possible birthdays stop, but there is one other curious note to be aware of, and that is that of the interplay between the Sun and the Moon. If he was born on October 29, 1814, he would have been born around the time of a full moon, but if he was born on April 11, 1815, he would have been born during the time of the new moon. Both of these fit his character, as people born around the time of the full moon tend to be more sensitive to the natural energies in the air, and usually have a tendency to be more psychic than most people. People born around the time of a new moon tend to be just as affected by the ambient energies in the air, too, but their paths tend to be a bit darker than most, which also

fits him. I draw attention to these two situations because it is uncommon to find both of those as possibilities in an astrological chart and both indicate that his soul picked an auspicious time to come into form. While the romantic in me would love to say that he was born around Halloween 1814, this timeframe doesn't hold up as well under scrutiny as the April 11, 1815 date, but it is very curious to note.

I hope this hasn't been too technical on the astrological side of things, but I do feel that at least some of this was necessary to walk you through the methodology that I used to arrive at these conclusions. On a final note, thank you to Michelle Young who helped produce some of the astrological transits that I used while processing this information. I invite anyone interested in this case to see what they come up with, for I will be the first to admit that chart rectification is not a strength of mine, but having said that, some astrological common sense can be applied to deduce the astrological riddle that is the birth date of Dr. John Montanee.

(See *DrJohnVoodoo.com* for more information.)

Rev. Bill Duvendack
418 Ascendant
418ascendant.com

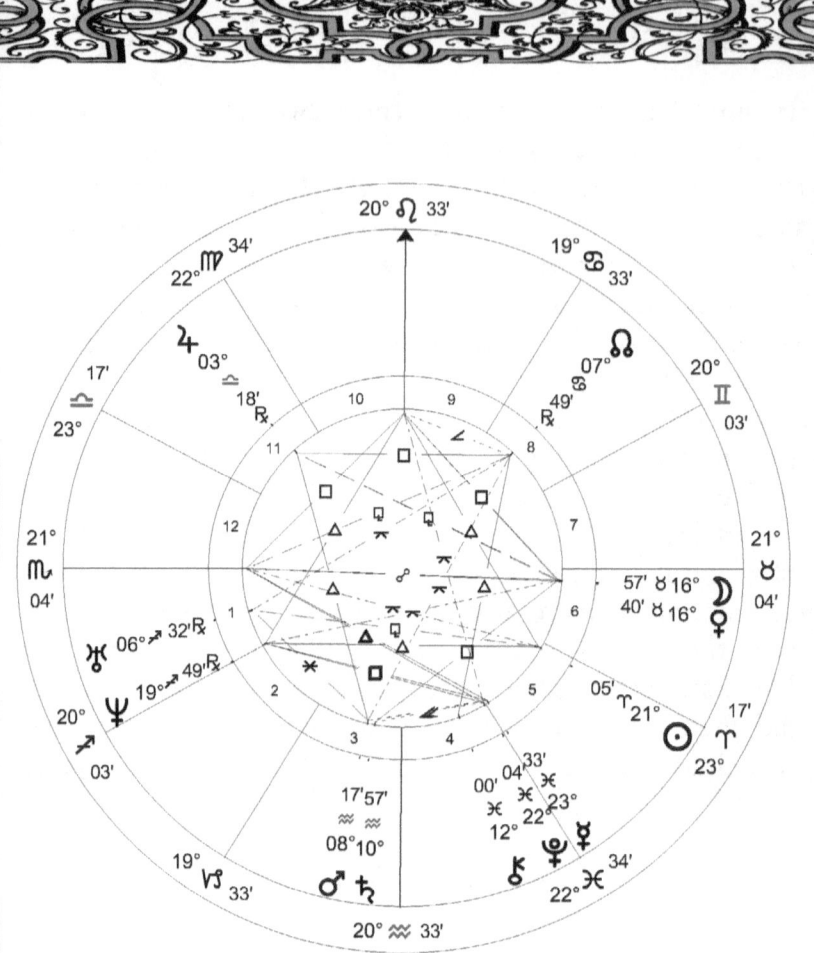

Dr. John Montanee's Astrological Natal Chart
by Rev. Bill Duvendack

Male Chart, April 11, 1815, NS Tues, 8:15 pm LMT +0:53:20
Simenti, Senegal, 13° N01'013° W20'
Geocentric, Tropical, Placidus, Mean Node, Rating: C

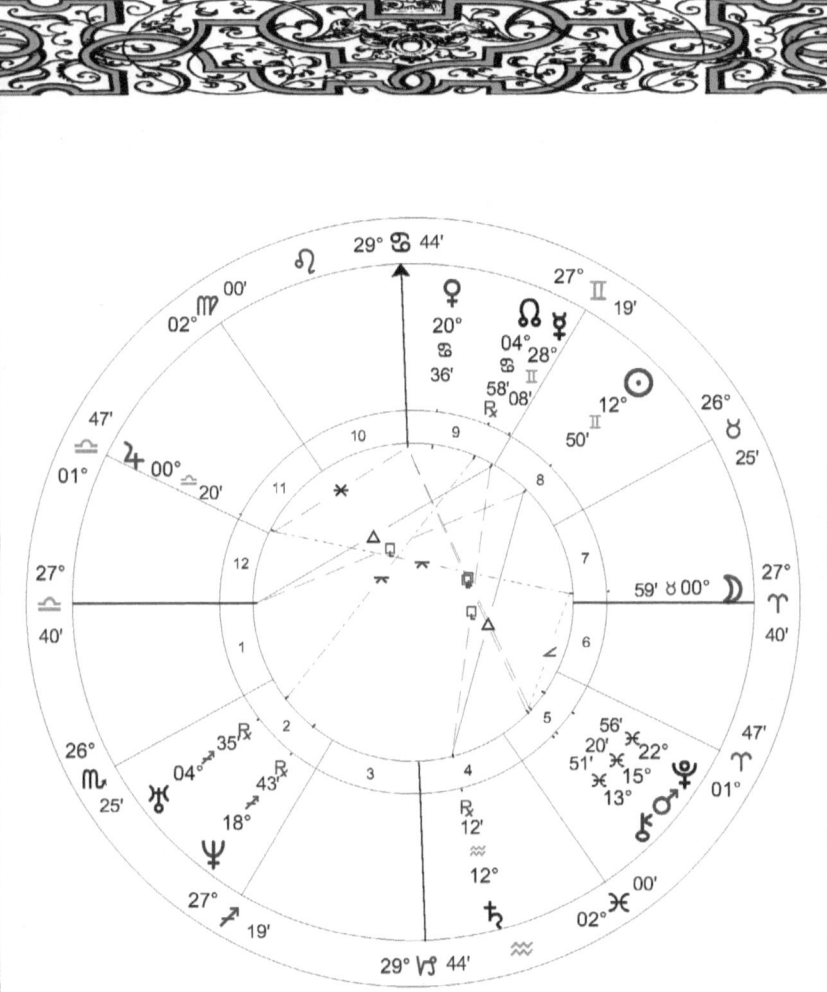

Dr. John Montanee's Marriage Progression Chart
by Rev. Bill Duvendack

Sec. Prog. SA in Long, Oct 20, 1868, NS Tues, 1:00 pm LMT +6:00:18
New Orleans, Louisiana, 29° N57' 16" 090° W04' 30"
Geocentric, Tropical, Placidus, Mean Node, Rating: C

Sonick Sigil: Drumming Dr. John's Name

© 2014 Vovin Lonshin and Louis Martinié

▽ :

Letter	X = High
	O = Rest
	+ = Low

Letter	1	2	3	4
A	X	X	X	
B	X	X		O
C	X	X		+
D	X	O	X	
E	X	O	O	
F	X	O		+
G	X	+	X	
H	X		O	+
I	X		+	+
J	O	X	X	
K	O	X	O	
L	O	X	+	
M	O	O		X
N	O	O		+
O			X	O
P	O		O	+
Q	O		+	
R	+		X	X
S	+	X		O
T	+	X		+
U	+		X	O
V	+		O	O
W		X	O	
X			X	+
Y		X	+	O
Z		X	+	+

The Spiritual Doctors of New Orleans

Doctor John
Doctor YaYa
Doctor Jack
Doctor Beauregard
Doctor Cat
Doctor Moses
Doctor Jim Alexander
Doctor Barkus
Doctor John – present
Doctor Charlie

From *Voodoo in South Louisiana* by Charles Gandolfo; New Orleans Historic Voodoo Museum, 1985.

The list of the early Doctors was compiled in life by Charles Gandolfo. There is a pristine symmetry and humility in adding his name to the list now, as he lies in the loving hands of the ancestors.

New Orleans Voodoo has a long history of male practitioners taking the title of Doctor and, perhaps in the future, more female voodoos will adopt the title. It is a designation of honor and respect maintained by the community in which the practitioner works. Anyone can call themselves Doctor; it is the community that decides

if the title sticks. John Montanee or simply John seems lacking, incomplete. Dr. John is music to the ears.

Snake Doctor, Indian Doctor, Spiritual Doctor, Conjure Doctor, Herb Doctor, and Root Doctor are all well set titles in the community of practitioners. Utu, of the Dragon Ritual Drummers, often uses Witch Doctor. In its blending of Wicca and Voodoo, it is an apt candidate to join the ranks of the above titles.

After all, it is good to remember that "clergy" as derived from the Greek word "kleros" refers to "lot" (as in "casting lots") or "that which is assigned by lot" and that sorcerer is literally one who casts lots.

An excellent and extensive treatment of the title Doctor as used by practitioners can be found in Harry Middleton Hyatt's monumental work, Hoodoo-Conjuration-Witchcraft-Rootwork; Western Publishing, 1935.

In Belated Refutation of the Appellation "Quack" as Applied to Dr. John.

(See pages 53-57, Document Number Four; page two.)
Doctor takes its origin from the Latin docere meaning "to teach." In archaic usage it referred to any person of great learning. Dr. John Montanee was of great learning in the use of conjures and herbs. Folklore has him as a teacher of Marie Laveau. "Marie Laveau was queen then and people say she learned a lot of tricks from old John Bayou." (Mr. Barnes, page 92, Folklore: Links and Pathways Section).

Doctor, always written with a capital "D," refers to the constellation Ophiuchus, The Serpent Bearer. There is a perfection here and an amazing symmetry with New Orleans Voodoo. The human figure depicted in starry

outline is Asclepios, a healer associated with the use of herbs. Here we have the original "snake doctor." The sacred serpent and New Orleans Voodoo are so tightly intertwined that to have described Dr. John Montanee as a snake doctor would have been much more accurate.

The caduceus, an emblem of the medical profession, is most commonly enlivened by two snakes and as such pays tribute to both Asclepios and Hermes (Mercury). The attribute of healing (Asclepios) is combined with commerce, eloquence, negotiation and the demeanor of trickster, the attributes of Hermes. Dr. John Montanee with his real estate dealings, coffeehouse, and other enterprises fits comfortably here.

With all due respect to Miss Ruthie the Duck Girl, quack has such a rude and ungentlemanly sound, one can only hope for the sake of close relatives that the Assistant Marshal who penned the document and appended quack to the Good Doctor's profession was not in the habit of voicing the word in his home.

Ending at The Beginning: Why? An Apologia

I thought this question best addressed at the end of the grimoire in that experimental practice is often much more interesting than mental explanations or speculations. Action not only speaks louder than words, it tends to define and qualify the words used to describe and explain its many times inevitable course. "Why" often presents itself as an afterthought.

Motivation is a complex matter somewhat like the onion with layer upon layer folding back to reveal an empty spot at its innermost core (Nema). To continue the analogy, I believe that presence emanates from the empty spaciousness of this core and translates into form when it comes into contact with the sensorium and mental apparatus of sentient beings. The form in this case consists of the various thoughts serving as motivations to provide offerings to Dr. John Montanee.

As a variety of people will be performing these conjures, it seems best to look at a variety of ways "why" can be approached and understood.

1. Due to Who we are:

WHY: Middle English, from Old English hwȳ, instr. case of hwæt…what.

WHAT: Middle English, from Old English hwæt, neuter of hwā...who

WHO: Middle English, from Old English hwā; akin to Old High German hwer, interrog. pron., who, Latin quis, Greek tis, Latin qui, relative pron....who
—Merriam Webster

Here is a trail in which "why" leads back to "what" which in turn collides with "who." There is an interesting kind of equivalency here between the "why" and the "who" of actions. Our working with Dr. John is motivated by who we are, by our very nature. We are conjurers by nature therefore we are drawn to perform the conjures of this grimoire.

This response is in the same box as, "I climbed the mountain K2 because I am a mountain climber." Here "by nature" can refer to everything from our karma to genetic inheritance to the fate or doom particular to us.

2. Due to a pure choice, we act for no reason:

Writers as diverse as Monsieur Camus (the gratuitous act) and Monsieur Hadit ("If Will stops and cries Why, invoking Because, then Will stops and does nought.") have pointed to the possibility of acting for no reason. Actions motivated by reasons are very unstable. Remove the reason and the doing collapses. The performance of the action depends on the reason(s) for the action and if the reasons are found faulty then the action ceases. In example, if the practitioner chooses to perform the conjures because she loves Dr. John and wants to care for him as a wife on every

Thursday of the week, then if a partner in the Visible World is found who objects the performance of the conjures could very well be abandoned. To choose to do the conjures for no reason imparts a much greater stability. "Why" is most functional in only the most straightforward of situations (I am fixing the plumbing because the loo won't flush).

3. The joy of the act:

The motivation here is found in an elated mental state brought on by the act of the doing the conjures. That action, in itself, is enjoyable. Performing the conjures brings the practitioner joy regardless of the result of the conjures. I often begin drumming for a rite because I want to call the loa. This "because" quickly transforms into the joy inherent in playing the drum with no thought of result. The drumming then takes on a depth and the loa are much more apt to come.

4. Curiosity:

This is the same kind of feeling that leads one to explore the neighborhood in which one lives. Who are the neighbors and what do they do? Our immediate neighborhood extends deeply into the Invisible Worlds. The spirits, loa, and Dr. John are our neighbors. What does Dr. John Montanee like to wear? What does he like to eat? In what relationship to Marie Laveaux does he now find himself?

Experimentation and investigation based on curiosity is deeply rewarding to us and to a variety of other sentient beings.

5. Being Told to Perform the Conjure / Being Told Not to

Perform the Conjure:

Here the motivation is perceived as external. The practitioner acts at the request/order of another being. Spiritual action based on an external authority, while deeply suspect, has its place and it may be helpful, particularly at the beginning of an enterprise or conjure.

6. Compassion:

All of us have needs and wants. All sentient beings in the Visible and Invisible Worlds have needs and wants. A Mother/Father feeds and cares for their children. A friend shares food and comfort with other friends. A voodoo shares what they have with the loa. Here the conjures are performed from a deep wisdom that perceives needs and wants in Dr. John and recognizes those same wants and needs in one self. Caring for Dr. John is cognizant with caring for oneself.

Dr. John may not be a perfected spirit. Ah! We all have our faults. I must confess that I have friends in the Visible World who just may be less than perfect. Still, recognizing myself in many of their less than perfect actions, I work for their benefit. The practitioner cares for, calls, and makes requests of the loa. It is good to remember that we are all microcosims and as such we can only find a final refuge, the final point from which being originates within our selves.

7. The Drum:

Dr. John is a patron of ritual drummers. All who are drummers or who love the drum hear its voice in the conjures. The drum has few patrons in the Invisible World.

Dr. John fills a needed position in the web that stretches between and deeply into the Visible and Invisible Worlds.

On a Personal Note

I am a creature of balance. I perform the conjures from a position that balances each of the above "whys" with each with the others. I love, honor , and respect the middle path. Too much or too little of any of the elements in my life lead me into a boredom against which "even gods struggle in vain (Nietzsche)".

Journeying in a rocket ship serves as an example of the value of the middle path. Say that black holes peak my interest and I want to physically travel into one. I purchase a rocket and locate my body snugly in its cone. Fuel is a major issue. I decide to use $AF-M_{315}$ as a propellant. I realize that too rich a mixture causes the rocket to explode in a fine pyrotechnic display and I am left in a number of crisp, little pieces every one of which still wondering about what it feels like to enter a black hole. Too poor a mixture of fuel and the rocket ship meanders slowly up only to quickly fall to the earth in a pile of rubble.

Of these two, I would prefer the beautiful fiery display but now the third alternative; the balanced middle way presents itself. Here I supply the mixture of fuel necessary to escape the earth and journey through wondrous regions of space. A balanced mixture, not too rich and not too poor. As I planned, there is sufficient fuel to come within reach of the event horizon of the black hole but not enough to offer any possibility of retuning to earth or remaining alive for long. All is well done. I approach the horizon and my interest is awe fully sated. Every thing and no thing

flash, blend , make a point (Kether) and . .I hope I have made a point about balance and the middle way.

The telling is often in the doing so I will recount notes from a short spiritual visit.

I enter St. Louis No. 1 and walk. The street is behind me. I cross the threshold of the graveyard and move into the quiet of the ancestors. A thank you to Marie Laveaux. So many looking. There is Dr. John's tomb. Alone.

I kneel and place my forehead on the tomb. My mind stops. A heaviness enters into my head. No room for thought or purpose. Habit remains. The habitual performance of the conjures has prepared me for this oft repeated pilgrimage.

The conjures make no sense. Words are gone. Only the deepest sense of the conjures remains. I am a part and all is a part of me. My world is larger. I carry another with me in my head.

I serve Dr. John Montanee. A conjure jar with earth from St. Roch Cemetery is emptied onto the tomb. Coffee is poured on to the earth. It spreads and seeps into the worn concrete. A pile of small stones to Manman Bridgette is assembled on the flat tomb. A Louisiana agate falls from the heap of stones. I know what is wanted next time. A woman seeks me out with questions. Words return. An I returns. The woman is on a mission. She shows me photo graphs of the Weeping Angel in the Metairie Cemetery. It is oddly important to her that I see and know of this angel. I leave the cemetery in a state of "no difference." I simply do what I do from habit, one action leading inevitably into another. The state gradually dissipates and I return to the Visible World with a self grown larger, more complete.

New Orleans: A Voodoo Pilgrimage

Pilgrimage is a layer of experience which lies a bit apart from what is usually done or sought on a journey. It is an extended act of Will that both guides and informs actions and their accompanying thoughts. It brings a depth to the experiences of the journey and a benefit which penetrates the trip's temporal and spatial boundaries reaching into the fabric of the pilgrim's daily life. Succinctly put, it acts to both invoke the sacred into the World and to evoke the sacred from the World. It anchors the Invisible to the Visible World in a sensual fest of sight, sound, smells, touch, and movement.

This section of the grimoire provides suggestions in the areas of preparation, travel arrangements, places, and people to experience to solidify and enrich the voodoo's relationship with Dr. John. It is best not to rush in the preparation or while in New Orleans. Doing too much is as spiritually debilitating as the dullness engendered by doing too little. Greed for experience and laziness are two sides of the same coin and they both lead to a state of mind which misses and often trips over what is directly under foot and within reach.

An obstacle that often arises is waiting for a perfect time to begin the pilgrimage. Perfection is seldom found and often disappoints when it actually manifests. Make offerings to the loa of what you have in the present moment

and put one foot in front of another. The important thing is to make the pilgrimage. Remember you are going to what is often called the Big Easy. Trust in the loa and spirits. Relax in the knowledge that the loa travel with you.

Follow the road you have constructed for the journey and, at the same time, be open to guidance from the hands of the loa. Like a tree, stay rooted and bend with the winds. Meet what comes with open arms. As Hesse advises in his classic *Journey to the South*, stop to pay homage at each sacred spot you pass be it a temple or a magnolia tree in blossom.

Both respect and test all that you hear and see. Seek knowledge based in experience, not belief. Do not become too "hot," such mental heat tends toward believing everything that you think. A condition in which one's way is mistaken for *the* way rather than *a* way. Revelation is often more personal than general. Share your revelations as *a* truth rather than *the* truth. Failure in this area may lead to a horrible fate such as knowing the "true" burial place of Marie Laveau or Dr. John.

Conjures for the Pilgrimage

Bring a bit of earth (Body of the Ancestors), waters (Blood of the Ancestors), and small stones (Bones of the Ancestors / Manman Bridgette) from your home as a link to places of pilgrimage. Bring very small amounts particularly if you are flying domestically and overseas. A few grains do the trick.

The earth, water, and stone can be left at places as links between your home and the location visited. First ask permission from the living and the dead and then leave

some in each location. By the same token, as proper, bring back a bit of earth, water, and stone from each place visited. Earth from Congo Square is particularly powerful.

The Magick Mirror is a fine instrument for conjure. Expeditions into this mirror provide the voodoo with a wealth of experience and inspiration. On your pilgrimage wear a small mirror, perhaps embedded in an inconspicuous piece of jewelry, to reflect and to absorb images and presence from the places visited. Once home, the small mirror can be affixed facing into the back of a mirror large enough to enter on expeditions. This opens the road to travels into the essences of the places visited.

Offer a glass of water to Dr. John. Change the water as warranted. When the water is refreshed, the water from which he drank can be used for scrying into the upcoming pilgrimage.

Preparation

Do what you can. Trust in the loa and spirits. The important thing is to make the pilgrimage.

Read all that you can find by Madame Barbara Trevigne and Carolym Morrow Long. They are main sources on Dr. John. *Vodou Visions* is an excellent work by a major vodou Manbo in New Orleans initiated in Haiti. *The New Orleans Voodoo Tarot* provides a good overall introduction to many of the loa. Dr. John holds the position of Magus in the deck and is described as "traveling the starry road to the position of loa." The bibliography lists these and other relevant titles.

Maegdlyn has extensive knowledge of Dr. John and was instrumental in the construction of this grimoire. She

is available for questions relating to your pilgrimage and navigating the culture of New Orleans. She also presents sessions on Dr. John Montanee and on this grimoire. She can be contacted at: maegdlyn@gmail.com.

Do readings and conjures to explore what will become available during the pilgrimage. Offer fresh water to Dr. John. Make offerings to your ancestors and to the Oguns. Ask your ancestors to travel with you. Ask the Oguns to protect you in your travels.

Travel

Be extra watchful if you plan your pilgrimage to coincide with hurricane season. Especially through late summer and early fall.

Aero Planes - Most expensive during festivals, especially the Mardi Gras. Cost to and from the airport is a factor to consider.

MegaBus - About 250 usd round trip within 1000 miles of New Orleans. Connections can be a bit complicated due to lack of direct routes.

Auto Mobile – Good for mobility within the city. Before the Storm (Hurricane Katrina) you didn't have to obey too many of the traffic laws, they could be viewed as good suggestions to be followed if you were too tired or otherwise unable to think for yourself. Now, regrettably, they are more strictly enforced. At least we still have our drive through Daiquiri shops. Watch where you park, especially in the French Quarter. The meter maids are voracious. Tuesday

and Thursday mornings see street cleaning in the Quarter and attendant towing.

ON FOOT – Baron Sylvia of the Ozark Voodoo Temple once walked hundreds of miles to New Orleans on pilgrimage. Time, two shoes, and many band aids are essential.

ACCOMMODATIONS

The city and surrounding parishes offer a variety of accommodations. The two most relevant to spiritual journeying are:

MAISON DE LA LUNE NOIR (in New Orleans)
Alternative, affordable lodging for the spiritual traveler, musician, and artist. (maison.blackmoon7.com) The Maison is run by my companion, Mishlen Linden, artist and author of *Typhonian Teratomas*. I routinely invite her guests to open rituals and drum rites/sessions. Contact: mishlenlinden@gmail.com. To view some of her art see mishlenlinden.com.

GRYPHON'S NEST (69 miles out of New Orleans, about an hour and a half drive)
This is the only site for alternative spirituality festivals in Louisiana. It is an excellent place to come into first hand contact with the spirits of the swamps and bayous. There is a 100 foot pathway leading out into a swamp. A fine place to be around the midnight hour.
Cliff runs Gryphon's Nest, heads a coven, and is a major supporter of our community. Camping and rooms available. Large heated pool. Contact: gryphonsnestcampground.com.

Into the Gumbo Of Particular Importance: People and Places

A sacrament is an outward sign of an internal state. New Orleans is inwardly a city populated by spirits and outwardly a city pregnant with possibilities which show themselves as people, places, and things.

See the Bibliography for detailed information on books noted in this section.

Congo Square
700 N. Rampart Street

This is the center of New Orleans in its role as the City of Spirits. Folklore has Dr. John drumming and calling the loa here. Walk in the thick mist of folklore and history.

Madame Barbara Trevigne

Madame has lectured, presented, and published extensively in venues too numerous to mention. She is a visual/performing artist, author, playwright, cultural historian, and New Orleans preservationist. Her historical reenactments of Marie Leveaux as a LSUE Performing Arts Series Artist are legendary in and of themselves. If your pilgrimage brings you to town during one of her presentations it is a spiritual experience not to be missed. Of particular note is the following award received by Madame:

LA Creole Member, Barbara Trevigne, being honored for her work.
From: Pat Schexnayder, President, LA Creole (Louisiana

Creole Research Association, Inc.)

I am proud to make the following announcement:
In recognition of the efforts of the Government of France toward the City of New Orleans, in particular the Femme, Femme, Femme exhibit at the New Orleans Museum of Art, L'Alliance Francaise de la Nouvelle-Orleans is honoring Trois Femmes of the Arts on May 11, 2007. Among the honorees is our own LA Creole member, Madame Barbara Trevigne, Artist, Playwright, and Storyteller.

Being honored with Madame Trevigne are Mme. Sharon Litwin, Senior vice-President, External Affairs, Louisiana Philharmonic Orchestra and Mme. Phyllis Taylor, Chairman and President of Patrick Taylor Foundation, Patron of the Arts.

This is a great honor not only for Barbara but for the Creole Culture she so passionately and admirably represents. Congratulations, Barbara. We are very proud of you.

NEW ORLEANS VOODOO SPIRITUAL TEMPLE/CULTURAL CENTER
828 N. Rampart Street

The Temple is located across Rampart Street from Congo Square. Priestess Miriam practices from the soul of New Orleans Voodoo. She is a skillful and sought after spiritual adviser and is visible in a number of the present Dr. John's music videos.

When visiting you can request to enter the Temple. Remember that this is a functioning temple, show honor and respect and the same will be returned by the spirits and loa.

Mishlen Linden once observed that to enter a temple is to enter the heart of its priestess or priest. The heart of

Priestess Miriam is both expansive and inclusive. I have been in service to the New Orleans Voodoo Spiritual Temple for over 25 year and have received much more than I have ever given. The Temple is a living inspiration.

Reverend Severina K.M. Singh

A tour of the swamps, bayous, and voodoo sites with her is both fascinating and enlightening. A pilgrimage she an I took together is recorded in *Voodoo at Café Puce*. neworleansvoodoocrossroads.com

New Orleans Healing Center/Island of Salvation Botanica

2372 Saint Claude Avenue in the Marigny

This is an important destination to experience the power of Voodoo in shaping the present New Orleans. Manbo Sallie Ann Glassman is strong in the lwa and inquiries can be made as to open rites. Her books, along with a wide variety of spiritual supplies are available. *Vodou Visions* is an important testimony, record, and sourcebook. I am honored to have worked with her on the *New Orleans Voodoo Tarot*. One memory is of her dog Loa trying to snatch offerings to the loa.

Luther Grey

From The Congo Square Foundation to Bamboula 2000, Luther Gray is an organizing force in the community. Mishlen Linden and I attended Sunday Congo Square Drum Sessions in the late 1980's and he continues to conduct them to this day. Catch him and hisw sessions if you can.

Starling Books

1022 Royal Street in the French Quarter

Owners Rev. Claudia Williams and Jan Spacek have maintained this cornerstone of Quarter occultism for decades. A large variety of occult supplies and books are available. Starling maintains an occult library and Museum replete with rare books.

Jan's knowledge on a wide range of occult and literary topics is exceptional. Ask Rev. Claudia about her personal experience with Dr. John as noted in this grimoire (page 130) and have her sign her very well received book of relevant and useful conjures; *Manifesting Magick with Vèvès and Sigils*.

F&F Botanica
801 N. Broad Street

F&F has been in New Orleans long before the pyramids were built in Egypt. It has a large selection of spiritual supplies and an abundance of atmosphere.

Historic Voodoo Museum
724 Dumaine Street in the French Quarter

This is the museum Claudia refers to in Voices of the Community (page 129). Jerry Gandolfo knows more about New Orleans Voodoo than any other living person I have met. If you are going on a tour, I would recommend him as a superbly informed guide.

His brother Charles, now with the ancestors, was a champion for voodoo long before it was either fashionable or lucrative. His assistance and offers of work have helped many conjure workers/card readers in the city. I have drummed for many rituals with John T. His calm nature and love of snakes allows him to work with some of the largest serpents I have seen outside of a serepentarium. I

was happy to be in a rite with him on Congo Square to honor Voodoo Charlie after his passing.

CABAL TAMBOUR/LOUIS MARTINIE
Contact me at: drjohn@drjohnvoodoo.com for sessions, rites, and events.

Frequent drum sessions on Thursday nights in New Orleans. I often travel to give sessions on New Orleans Voodoo, Dr. John Montanee, the conjures in this grimoire, and confirmations in the Order of Service/Drumming developed at the New Orleans Voodoo Spiritual Temple over a five year period of Thursday night open rituals.

NEW ORLEANS PHARMACY MUSEUM
514 Chartres Street in the French Quarter

This is an important link to the apothecaries that existed in New Orleans during Dr. John Montanee's time. You may want to take a note book to record a variety of information on healing in the eighteen hundreds.

SEVEN SISTERS OF ALGIERS
800 Brooklyn in Algiers across the Mississippi from central New Orleans

If a visit is in the cards, the trip is worthwhile. Spiritual supplies are available and there is a museum on the premises. Seven Sisters of Algiers has an amazing drum whose head is secured by bones that I am honored to have played. Algiers is known as "Hoodoo City."

SAINT LOUIS NO.1 CEMETERY
Located on the north side of Basin Street within easy walking distance of Congo Square. Walk down the aisle to the left of Madame Marie Laveau's tomb. The Good

Doctor's tomb is located directly behind the pyramid.

This is the folkloric resting place of Dr. John Montanee (pages 110-114) and a center point of any pilgrimage honoring the Good Doctor. Spend time here. Touch the tomb and be touched by it. A suggestion is to buy some water from the water sellers standing at the entrance to the cemetery. Pour the water on Dr. John's tomb. Leave something consecrated with your sweat or saliva as a link.

Saint Roch Cemetery
1725 Saint Roch Avenue

Saint Roch hits Saint Claude at the Healing Center. Ignore the benign dispute and proceed toward St. Roch Market, the large building across St. Claude from the Healing Center. The cemetery is about five blocks up the street from the Market.

Often referred to as The Voodoo Cemetery. Time and the Storm (Hurricane Katrina) has erased the memory and possibly the location in the cemetery of Dr. John's mortal remains. The Chapel Reliquiry contains objects left by people touched by the power of St. Roch and other spirits. A token can be left if you are so inclined.

There is a basin with water to the left as you enter the Cemetery. Leave your hand print on the stone and take some of the water with you. Pour it as an offering to Dr. John where you feel his presence.

Saint Louis Cathedral
615 Pere Antoine Alley

Dr. John was buried with the rites of the Roman Catholic Church. This is a church that celebrates the beauty and mysteries of life. A few prayers for the Good Doctor would not be amiss.

French Quarter / Jackson Square

There are many spirits here and they are best seen late at night without the crush of living beings. Use your street sense and walk the Quarter with them.

Mississippi River

The river cradles New Orleans in its mostly loving though at times overpowering arms. Its waters have been used to bless, anoint, and baptize. Reverend Severina K.M. Singh once told me that New Orleans Voodoo could be more properly called River Voodoo or Mississippi River Voodoo. Take some water and leave something for the river. The ancestors swim in its waves.

In addition to the above, the following are places of interest in the Quarter. There are many voodoo houses and locations in New Orleans. The above I know and frequent, those below may very well give a healing depth to your pilgrimage. When you leave New Orleans, there are even more to be found in the surrounding parishes. As I wrote at the beginning, you (and I) can't be everywhere and do everything. Let spirit guide you.

Voodoo Authentica
612 Dumaine Street

Owner Brandi makes a big effort to support local spiritual authors. Voodoofest sponsored by Voodoo Authentica which occurs around Halloween is an importantcommunity event.

Hex
1219 Decatur Street

Owner Christian Day is a strong supporter of Pagan

Pride and works toward unity of the spiritual community.

WITCHCRAFT SHOP
541 Rue Dumaine
   Charms, herbs, oils, and occult books.

MARIE LAVEAU'S HOUSE OF VOODOO
739 Bourbon Street
   Charms, herbs, oils, and occult books. In the center of the action on Bourbon.

BOTTOM OF THE CUP TEA ROOM
327 Chartres Street
   I dreampt of this establishment in detail a number of decades ago. It was as I had seen it in the dream and I, for some reason, never went back. Ah! The secrets that sleep on untraveled roads....someday.

"Pilgrimages never really begin or end. They surface and dive once again like shadowy whales into the same darkness that soothes the sharp angles of the flat I am in; the darkness that connects the flat to the windows, to the street, to the city, to me. There is no telling when or where these restless whales will once again surface into the world of days, months, and years."
— *Voodoo at Café Puce*, pg. 9.

Now let us end this section with a bit of balance from the dedicated (obsessive/compulsive) Mr. Hyatt:
"Ah don' need tuh go tuh New Orleans tuh learn nuthin." (*Informant from Memphis, Tennessee as quoted in* Hoodoo-Conjuration-Witchcraft-Rootwork; *Interviews Section: My*

conversations with Hoodoo Doctors, Harry Middleton Hyatt, vol.3, page 1,859.)

Bibliography

In the construction of this grimoire, I soon had to come to terms with the paucity of material on Dr. John when compared to the copious and well deserved amount of material on Marie Laveaux. The grimoire that you now hold in your hands is the first book to bring together a myriad of source, secondary, and tertiary material relevant to both the study of and the offering of service to Dr. John Montanee.

This bibliography is a seed that will be brought to fruition in digital form on DrJohnVoodoo.com. It is the beginning of an exhaustive list of books, documents, articles, audio recordings, and art directly focused in whole or in part on Dr. John or presenting a context for his mortal life and road to loa. The majority of the work cited here falls into the second category due to the small but nonetheless crucial amount of material on Dr. John.

Those interested in contributing to this important search for relevant material on Dr. John Montanee are most welcome and can contact us at DrJohn@DrJohnVoodoo.com.

Alvarado, Denise. *The Voodoo Doll Spellbook: A Compendium of Ancient and Contemporary Spells and Rituals.* San Francisco, CA, Weiser Books, 2014.

Alvarado, Denise and Doktor Snake. *The Voodoo Hoodoo SpellBook.* San Francisco, CA, Red Wheel/Weiser, 2011.

Alvarado, Denise and Madrina Angelique. *Workin' in da Boneyard.* Prescott Valley, AZ, Creole Moon Publications,

2012.

Asbury, Herbert. *The French Quarter.* New York, NY, Alferd A. Knopf, Inc., 1936 (Pocket Cardinal, New York, NY, 1967.)

Bodin, Ron. *Voodoo Past and Present* (Louisiana Life Series, No.5). Lafayette, LA, The Center for Louisiana Studies, University of Southwestern Louisiana, 1990.

Evans, Freddi Williams. *Congo Square: African Roots in New Orleans.* Lafayette, LA, Lafayette Press at University of Louisiana, 2011.

Fandrich, Ina Johanna. *Marie Laveau: The Mysterious Voodoo Queen.* New Orleans, LA, Garrett County Press, 2012.

Glassman, Sallie Ann and Martinié, Louis. *The New Orleans Voodoo Tarot.* Rochester, VT, Destiny Books, 1992.

Glassman, Sallie Ann. *Vodou Visions: An Encounter with Divine Mystery.* New York, NY, Villard, 2000.

Gandolfo, Charles Massicot. *Voodoo in South Louisiana.* New Orleans, LA, The New Orleans Historic Voodoo Museum, rev. ed. 1987.

Gandolfo, Charles and Gandolfo, Jerry. *Le Voodoo a là Nouvelle Orleans: A Strolling Tour of Voodoo in the Vieux Carré.* New Orleans, LA, New Orleans Historic Voodoo Museum, 1975.

Hall, Gwendolyn Midlo. *Africans in Colonial Louisiana: The*

Development of Afro-Creole Culture in the Eighteenth Century. Baton Rouge, LA, Louisiana State University Press, 1992.

Haskins, Jim. *Voodoo and Hoodoo.* New York, NY, Stein and Day, 1978.

Hearn, Lafcadio. *The Last of the Voudoos.* Harper's Weekly Magazine, New York, NY, Nov. 7, 1885.

Hurston, Zora Neal. *Mules and Men.* New York, NY, Harper Perennial Library, 1990 (orig. pub. 1935).

Hyatt, Harry Middleton. *Hoodoo-Conjuration-Witchcraft-Rootwork.* 5 vols. Hannibal, MO, Western Publishing Co., 1970-78.

Jacobs, Claude F. and Kaslow, Andrew J. *The Spiritual Churches of New Orleans.* Knoxville, TN, The University of Tennessee Press, 1991.

Johnson, Jerah. *Congo Square in New Orleans.* New Orleans, LA, Louisiana Landmarks Society, 1995.

Long, Carolyn Morrow. *A New Orleans Voudou Priestess: The Legend and Reality of Marie Laveau.* Gainesville, FL, University Press of Florida, 2006.
   Madame Lalaurie: Mistress of the Haunted House. Gainesville, FL, University Press of Florida, 2012.
   Spiritual Merchants: Religion, Magic and Commerce. Knoxville, TN, The University of Tennessee Press, 2001.
   Art cards by Carolyn Long include *Marie Laveau* (illustration for the cover of *A New Orleans Voudou Priestess*),

Tea with Marie, Two Maries, Blue Runner, Mater Dolorosa/Ezili Freda. All are related to Marie Laveau, New Orleans, and Voudou.

Martinié, Louis. *Waters of Return: The Aeonic Flow of Voudoo.* Cincinnati, OH, Black Moon Publishing, 1986.
  A Priest's Head, A Drummer's Hands. New Orleans, LA, and Cincinnati, OH, Black Moon Publishing, 2010.
  Talking to God with Food: Questioning Animal Sacrifice. New Orleans, LA, and Cincinnati, OH, Black Moon Publishing, 2012.

Saxon, Lyle and Tallant, Robert and Dryer, Edward. *Gumbo Ya-Ya: A Collection of Louisiana Folk Tales.* New York, NY, Bonanza Books, 1945.

Singh, Severina K.M. and Louis Martinié. *Voodoo at Café Puce.* New Orleans, LA, Black Moon Publishing, 2005.

Tallant, Robert. *Voodoo in New Orleans.* Gretna, LA, Pelican Publishing Company, 1990 (copyright by author, 1946).
  The Voodoo Queen. Gretna, LA, Pelican Publishing Company, 1983 (copyright by author, 1956).

Teish, Luisah. *Jambalaya: The Natural Woman's Book of Personal Charms and Practical Ritual.* San Francisco, CA, Harper & Row, 1985.

Toups, M. Oneida. *Magick High and Low.* Jefferson, LA, Hope Publications, 1975.

Trevigne, Madame Barbara. *Ball of Confusion: Célestin Glapion and the Glapion Family of Louisiana.* New Orleans,

LA, New Orleans Genesis, Genealogical Research Society, Vol. XLVIII, No. 192, October, 2010.

Numerous relevant articles, papers, lectures, and performances best accessed through a web search.

Ward, Martha. *Voodoo Queen: The Spirited Lives of Marie Laveau.* Jackson, MS, University Press of Mississippi, 2004.

Williams, Claudia. *Manifesting Magick with Vèvès and Sigils.* New Orleans, LA, and Cincinnati, OH, Left Hand Press. 2013.

INDEX

Selected entries of interest to be used in conjunction with the detailed contents page:

Abou, Pop, 92
Agwe, 16
Akoko, 22
Altar, Dr. John, 220
Anderson, Leafy, 102, 103
Angel, Holy Guardian, 13, 19
Asbury, Herbert, 102, 208
astrology, 102, 128, 174-177

Babalon Rising, 4, 124-128, 151, 152, 154, 155
Baleine, 16
Bamboula 2000, 200
Bamboula rhythm, 126, 146, 150
Barnes, Nathan, 92, 93, 184
Baron Cimetiere, 15
Baron le Croix, 15
Baron Samedi, 15
Bate Cabal, 11
Bayou St. John, 102, 132
Blanc dan-i, 121, 149
Bodin, Ron, 91, 208
Bönpo Dzogchen, 13
Bridgette, Manman, 13, 19, 149, 192, 194
Bright's disease, 78, 85, 156-158, 175, 176
Buddhas, 13, 90

Cabal Tambour, 202
Cliff (Gryphon's Nest), 4, 197

coconut oil, 110, 126
coffeehouse, 51, 52, 104, 185
connaissance, 9, 17-19
Contradino, Bob, 9
cooker, 11
Crowley, Aleister, 3, 104

Damballah la Flambeau, 17
dead loa, 4, 22
death certificate, 81, 85-87, 174-177
documents, historical
  (see historical documents)
drum (instrument), 92, 93, 107, 110, 118, 119, 121, 122, 124, 125, 138, 143, 144, 151, 154, 155, 170, 189, 190, 200, 202
drums, 29, 37, 110, 126, 146, 152, 155, 156
drum, djembe, 143
drum, black, 144
drum (to play), 118, 119, 121, 122, 126, 197, 202
drummed, 27, 91, 143, 201
drumming, 34, 91, 93, 119, 134, 137, 138, 143, 144, 146, 182, 189, 198, 202
drummers, 4, 38, 40, 93, 103, 107, 119-122, 124, 125, 131, 133, 144, 150, 152, 162, 184,

190, 199
drum loa, 122, 124, 125
Duvendack, Bill, 173, 179, 180, 181

Erzulie, 17

Falario, Linda 2, 4, 105, 109, 143, 212
Farber, Phil, 127, 128, 151
La Fete des Morts, 144
Florida Water, 126, 156
Fowler, Fred 2, 4
French Quarter, 133, 142, 196, 200-202, 204
French Quarter, The 102

Gandolfo, Charles, 130, 183, 208
Gandolfo, Jerry, 201, 208
Genesis, New Orleans, 78
Glapion (surname), 61, 78, 80-82, 85, 210
Glassman, Sallie Ann, 4, 11, 26, 103, 124, 125, 200, 208,
grammar, 9, 10, 21
graveyard dust, 15, 126
Gray, Luther, 200
gris gris, 134, 164, 168, 169
Gris Gris Lamp, 133
Grisgris, John, 94, 170
Gros Bon Ange, 13, 19
Gryphon's Nest, 4, 118, 119, 121, 197
Guedeh, baby, 152
Guedeh Nibo, 15
Guedeh la Flambeau, 17

Guin, Urwsula K. Le, 31
Gwenivere, 3

Healing Center, New Orleans, 200, 203
Hearn, Lafcadio, 78, 82, 85, 86, 94, 143, 144, 163, 170, 172, 174, 209
herb, 83, 97, 133, 135, 184
herbs, 17, 97, 100, 101, 134, 136, 184, 185, 199, 205
herbal, 34, 91, 94, 164
herbalist, 40, 85, 199
historical documents:
   Doc. 1: Transaction (with signature), 40-46
   Doc. 2: Dr. John signature, 47, 48
   Doc. 3: US Census of 1850, (coffeehouse, birth in Africa, finc. worth), 49-52
   Doc. 4: US Census of 1860 (occupation physician, "quack," children), 53-57
   Doc. 5: Collection District List, 1864, (occupation physician), 58, 59
   Doc. 6 Certificate of Marriage, 60, 61
   Doc. 7: Certificate of Death, 62, 63
   Doc. 8: Interment Record and Map of Cemetery, 64-66
   Doc. 9: Succession, 67-77
   Doc. 10: Ball of Confusion,

(article, organizes historical information) 78-88
Hoodoo, 101, 134, 135, 170, 184, 202, 206
Hoodoo-Conjuration-Witchcraft-Rootwork, 206
Hyatt, Harry Middleton, 205, 206
hypertension, 158, 159

insect loa, 12, 127
Isis, 22, 26, 28

Jacobs, Claude F., 102, 209
Jambalaya, 93, 210
Joey, 4, 150
John, Dr. (Montanee, as per his signature, p. 47)
Names:
Montanet, Jean 94
Montanée, 78
Montaneé, 78
Montane, 56, 59, 61
Montaine, 78
Montanent, 78
Montaigne, John 93
Titles:
Bayou John, 94
DJ, 3, 123, 125, 128
Hoodoo John, 94
Jean Bayou, 94
Jean La Ficelle (a French bread similar to a baguette but much thinner), 94
Jean Grisgris, 94
Jean Latinié (possibly "Latin"), 94
Jean Macaque (a new world monkey), 94
Jean Racine (a celebrated French dramatist, late sixteen hundreds), 94
John Bayou, 94
Voudoo John, 94
John, Dr. (The Night Tripper/Malcolm "Mac" Rebennack), 4, 52, 104, 118, 132, 149
John, Father, 103
John T., 201

K-Doh, Ernie, 104
Kaslow, Andrew J., 102, 209
Katrina, Hurricane, 39, 66, 116, 139, 140, 143, 196, 203
kidney (failure), 157, 158, 159
Kraig, Don, 128
Kufaru, 144

Laveau, Marie, 10, 37, 38, 51, 61, 77, 90-93, 102, 105, 110, 121, 122, 139, 140, 141, 164, 184, 189, 192, 194, 202, 205, 208-211
Laveaux, Marie, 82, 85, 164, 168, 170, 207
Laveau II, Marie, 92, 93
Legba, 17, 146
Legba la Flambeau, 17
Linden, Mishlen, 3, 11, 105, 110, 122, 143, 149, 197, 199, 200
Litany to the Good Doctor, 106, 107

Loa, 1, 4, 9, 12, 18, 22, 25, 29, 31, 33, 38, 39, 90, 93, 103-105, 107, 121, 122, 124-127, 130, 133, 146, 150, 155, 172, 189, 190, 193-195, 198, 199, 200, 207
loadstone(s), 11, 13-20, 136
Long, Carolyn Morrow, 4, 38, 46, 48, 51, 79, 86, 102, 120, 195, 209
Lwa, 200

Maegdlyn, 3, 38, 122, 127, 128, 148, 151, 195, 196
Magick: High and Low, 210
Magick Mirror, 14, 26-28, 195
Maison Blanche, 92
Maison de la Lune Noir, 197
Margaret, Priestess, 129-131
Martinié, Louis, 1, 2, 3, 11, 26, 103, 104, 118, 124, 125, 132, 143, 146, 148, 154, 162-164, 172, 182, 202, 208, 210
Marty (Dr. Marty Laubach), 4, 128
Millipede, Ti Jean, 15
Miriam, Priestess, 4, 128, 132, 139, 143, 145, 154, 199
Mississippi, 86, 115, 121, 132, 149, 202, 204
Mississippi River Voodoo, 204
Montanee, Dr. John (see John, Dr.)
Morts, 126, 144

Neal, 128

Nema, 4, 187
Nephritis, 158, 159
New Orleans Genesis, (see *Genesis, New Orleans*)
New Orleans Voodoo Spiritual Temple, 4, 29, 118-122, 139, 143, 145, 199, 202
New Orleans Voodoo Tarot, 11, 26, 103, 123-125, 142, 195, 200, 208
Nietzsche, 191
night sky (Dr. John looking for signs/communications), 123, 124
Norma, 118

Ogun, 17
Olokun, 16
Oneida, 210
Order of Service, 121, 122, 126, 164, 172, 202
Osiris, 22, 26, 28, 105, 117
Oswan, Priest, 29, 127, 143
Ozark Voodoo Temple, 4, 197

Paris, Widow, 82, 162
Parasol (herb to cure yellow fever), 101
Patrick, 3
Prayer by Dr. John (Mac Rebennack), 118
A Priest's Head, A Drummer's Hands, 104, 151, 163, 164, 172, 210

quack (as applied to Dr. John),

56, 85, 184, 185
quack (refutation), 184

Radcliff, Jessica, 149
Rebennack, Mac (Dr. John), see John, Dr.
red palm oil, 110, 126, 138
rock(s), black, 11, 20, 149
Roy, Badal, 123
Ruthie the Duck Girl, Miss, 185

Saint John's Eve, 20
St. Louis Cemetery No. 1, 34, 103, 105, 139, 140
Saint Jude, 103
St. Roch Cemetery, 34, 66, 85, 87, 111, 113, 114, 149, 192, 203
Senegal (birthplace Dr. John), 95, 98, 100, 131, 143, 144, 169, 171, 174-178, 180
Senegalese, 93
Sergeant, Denny, 21
Simbi, 17
Simbi la Flambeau, 17
la Siréne, 16
slave, 95, 102, 143, 171
slave (Dr. John as slave), 93-96, 100-102, 143, 165, 168, 169
slave(holders) (Dr. John as slaveholder), 80, 94, 98, 166
spider loa, 12
spider(s), 12, 30
Spiritual Churches of New Orleans, The, 102, 209
Spiritual Doctors of New Orleans, 7, 183

star, 128, 151
Starwood, 4, 120-122, 132, 146
success (ancient usage), 13

Tallant, Robert, 92, 93, 104, 210
Teish, Luisah, 93, 94, 210
Tibet(an), 13, 21, 27, 89
Ti Bon Ange, 19
Ti Zaraguin, 12
Tomb, Dr. John (painting), 2, 109, 143, 144
Trevigne, Madame Barbara, 4, 38, 61, 63, 77, 78, 86, 88, 102, 195, 198, 199, 210

Voodoo in New Orleans, 93
Voodoo, Past, and Present, 91
Voodoo Queen, The, 93
Voudoos, The Last of the, 94-101, 170, 174, 209

water, a favored offering to Dr. John, 123, 153, 155-159, 203
Waters, Mamie, 126
Waters of Return, 18, 210
Wicca(n), 119, 184
witchcraft, 95, 100, 171, 184, 205, 206
whorehouse (coffeehouse, Dr. John and Dr. John (Mac) relative), 104
womb, 18, 20

Zayin, 4

Other Publications by
Black Moon Publishing

The Faces of Babalon
A Compilation of Women's Voices
by Mishlen Linden, Linda Falorio, Soror Chen, Nema
and Raven Greywalker

Typhonian Teratomas: The Shadows of the Abyss
by Mishlen Linden

Waters of Return: The Aeonic Flow of Voudoo
by Louis Martinié

A Priest's Head, A Drummer's Hands
New Orleans Voodoo Order of Service
by Louis Martinié

Talking to God With Food: Questioning Animal Sacrifice
by Louis Martinié

The Priesthood: Parameters and Responsibilities by Nema

Maatian Meditations and Considerations
A Continuation of Past Writings on "She Who Moves"
by Nema

Feather and Firesnake by Nema

Wings of Rapture by Nema

Enochian Temples by Benjamin Rowe

The Book of the Seniors by Benjamin Rowe

The 91 Parts of the Earth by Benjamin Rowe

Gilles de Rais: The Banned Lecture by Aleister Crowley

BLACKMOONPUBLISHING.COM

Dr. John Altar

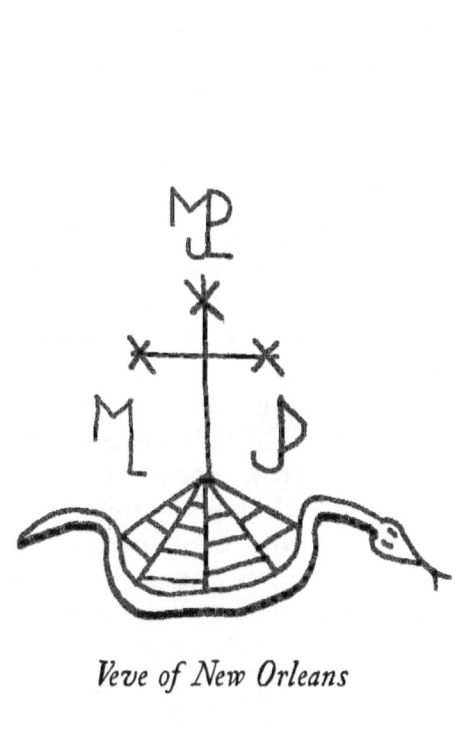

Veve of New Orleans

Dr. John Montanee, A Grimoire
The Path of a New Orleans Loa,
Resurrection in Remembrance

The first book length publication celebrating the life and times of the first Dr. John (birth circa 1815 - passing 1885), this publication contains conjures meant to offer Dr. John the opportunity to become a fully present loa in today's world.

History and folklore have Dr. John filling many posts. He was a freeman of color reputed to be a contemporary of Marie Laveaux in the voodoo on Congo Square, a New Orleans conjure man, drummer, herbalist, physician, and spiritual Doctor as well as having a coffeehouse and dealing in real estate. He was a man worth knowing and is a spirit worth working with.

Reprints of the actual historical documents include a contract with Dr. John's signature, his Marriage Certificate, his Death Certificate, and various censuses from the period providing important keys to his life. Folkloric sources of beliefs about Dr. John, both verbal and written, are extensively treated. An index and a bibliography add to the book's ease of use.

A unique feature of the book consists of experiments, explorations, experiences, investigations, teachings, and conjures by current members of the spiritual community which are provided to bring the reader closer to Dr. John and Dr. John closer to the reader. The collection of this material is ongoing through DrJohnVoodoo.com and the reader is encouraged to participate in this great work.

This book is a comprehensive reference for the study of Dr. John as well as the offering of service to the Good Doctor. So often it is heard that little is published on Dr. John. Now that is no longer the case.

> "Do the conjures. Then listen as once dry dust takes on a new life. The facts of history are the bones. Folklore is the flesh. Conjure is the spirit. Dr. John will speak to you."

www.ingramcontent.com/pod-product-compliance
Lightning Source LLC
Chambersburg PA
CBHW030854170426
43193CB00009BA/607